never
give in

never
give up

never give in

never give up

CARLANA STONE LAWSON
&
JOHN DI RIENZO

This publication is designed to provide accurate and authoritative information in regard to the subject matter covered. It is sold with the understanding
that the publisher is not engaged in rendering legal, accounting, or other
professional service. If legal advice or other expert assistance is required,
the services of a competent professional person should be sought.—*From
a Declaration of Principles Jointly Adopted by a Committee of the American Bar
Association and a Committee of Publishers and Associations*

Published by Sourcebooks, Inc.
P.O. Box 4410, Naperville, Illinois   60567-4410
(630) 961-3900
FAX: (630) 961-2168
www.sourcebooks.com

Library of Congress Cataloging-in-Publication Data

Lawson, Carlana Stone.
  Never give in, never give up / Carlana Stone Lawson and John Di Rienzo.
    p. cm.
  1. Life skills. 2. Conduct of life. 3. Life change events. 4. Lawson, Carlana
Stone. 5. Paraplegics — United States — Biography. I. Di Rienzo, John. II.
Title.

HQ2037.L39 2005
306.73'4'08730973 — dc22

                                        2005019872

Printed and bound in the United States of America.
POD 10 9 8 7 6 5 4 3

Contents

CHAPTER 1

Tragedy Strikes

• •

"Carlana Stone...you have the finest ass in Louisiana."

"Shut up, James," I said with one of those cat-like smirks that showed both annoyance and an underlying appreciation. *Tell me something I don't know,* I thought as I felt his eyes burning a hole through my skirt. Being a gymnast, my life was all about strength and performance, and of course, the killer bod that came with it.

I adored James, my boyfriend during my junior year in high school. He was so cool and beautiful, and that night he had managed to get us invited to the opening of the Stark Club in Dallas. The timing was perfect; my parents were out of town. With teenage zeal, we jumped into the car and drove off for a big night out with our friends Laura and Bobby. We were young, good-looking, and on our way to one of the hottest events in the South. Everything seemed perfect. But somewhere a clock was ticking: one that I could neither hear nor see but whose hour hand was slowly moving towards me and from which there was no escape.

What a great night. I was so happy. I remember I wore one of the shortest miniskirts that the 80s could bear. I recall walking into the club when we arrived. It was modern and sexy, with coed bathrooms and mirrored ceilings. James held me close and we danced the night away. The air felt good on my legs. I had no idea that I would be forever connected with the opening night of that club.

The evening was a blur of drinking and dancing and the night culminated with laughs and nightcaps. At about 2:30 a.m. we piled into the car, exhausted and sated after our decadent night. For a moment, we all stopped to consider whether it was wise to drive the three hours home to Shreveport in our condition. But in the end, Bobby drove and Laura rode shotgun. It was late but I still had time to make it home before my parents returned. My dad was at a speaking engagement and he and my mom would not be home until the next morning. I felt like Cinderella sneaking back from the ball and was extremely content as I snuggled up against James for the ride home.

In hindsight, my contentedness came as much from the great evening we had just shared as it did from being happy with who and what I was. I was seventeen and I had a very strong sense of self. I was the girl at the center of everything: the president of the student body, a competitive gymnast, a cheerleader. I was going places and saw a future wide open for the taking. I drifted off to sleep wrapped in a blanket of confidence and certainty, unaware that my witching hour was swiftly approaching.

The next thing I remember was the screaming. Bobby had jumped out of the car and started to shout, "Tell them I swerved to avoid a dog! Please!"

Laura jumped out and then James followed her. "Get out! Get out!" someone was yelling.

There was no fire but my legs were burning. I was still not quite sure what had happened. I was fighting for air. But even in my delirium, I felt fear and I knew that I had to get out of there. My first thought was about my parents and how upset they were going to be with me. James was shouting at me to get out of the car. I pulled myself together and went for the door. But something wasn't right. My legs wouldn't move. I tried again and still nothing. My lower half was totally numb.

"I can't moo-ve!" I yelled in frustration. *I can't breathe, what's going on?* I thought. I remember pulling myself up on the handle above the door.

"Stay put! Don't move!" James was screaming back, realizing something was wrong.

The world was spinning. I gasped for breath and struggled to get myself up, but my body wouldn't listen. The body that I had trained so hard, that took me safely across balance beams, and made me the center of so much attention, just sat there. James came running towards the car.

"Don't move!" he said.

I knew there was no fire so I tried to stay put and keep focused. Whenever I moved there was a stabbing pain in my back. What followed was a huge blur of paramedics and strangers in my face telling me to lie still. At that point I had no choice but to listen.

The next thing I remember I was lying on my back in a strange place that was horribly white and sterile. A doctor stood over me. A nurse was there too. Just an hour before I had been content and carefree in my boyfriend's arms. And then I saw Poosie. She was my brother-in-law's aunt and lived in a town nearby in Texas. Someone had called her. I was throwing up into a container that she was holding. I remember the jolting pain in my back every time I would vomit. It was excruciating; everything was happening so fast. Then, in this cold, antiseptic place, a man entered. He was someone I had never seen, yet he approached me as if we had met before. He was clearly a doctor. With a practiced calmness, he sat by me, looked me straight in the eye, and explained that I had broken my back.

I tried to process the words. Then he added that my legs were paralyzed and that I might never walk again.

Paralyzed? I thought. *Did he just say paralyzed? It can't be that easy. An hour before I was dancing.*

"Your spinal cord has been damaged," he said.

An hour before I was a cheerleader. I wanted my mom and dad. I wanted to know why this was happening to me.

Terrible things can happen at any time. To any one of us. Sometimes we can see them coming and other times they can hit us like a line drive and shatter everything we know in one seemingly endless moment. Somewhere along a stretch of highway between Dallas, Texas, and Shreveport, Louisiana, I lost the girl who walked through life with casual ease. I joined the legions of people who find themselves asking, "Oh, God, why me?"

In the days and weeks after a shock is absorbed and the resulting crisis begins to abate comes the inevitable question, "What will become of me?" At that moment we hold our lives in our own hands. How we respond is the ultimate measure of success or failure.

In this book, I will share with you my story and how I responded to a life-altering accident. In the almost twenty years since my accident, I have achieved more than I could ever have hoped to, walking or not. I have lived overseas, worked as a TV reporter, produced primetime TV shows in Hollywood, and even fallen in love.

The journey back from tragedy was not always easy or painless. It was, however, filled with revelations: insights that hold the key to overcoming obstacles and realizing your true potential.

I hope that my story and my experience will offer you tools that you can use in your own life and perhaps make you a little wiser than I was when I was seventeen and ready to take on the world.

CHAPTER 2

Rehab: Redefining the Self

Not Without a Fight: The Struggle to Save the Self

For ten days I remained too fragile to be moved from the intensive care unit of the hospital in Texas that received me on the night of the accident. But I was eventually transferred to a rehab where I would focus on getting my legs to work again.

When I arrived at the rehab I remember being wheeled down a long white hall on a gurney. I couldn't even sit up yet. As I was pushed about, I could barely see the world around me. For the first time in my life, I couldn't see ahead of myself. I felt powerless. All I could see were the walls beside me, towering upwards, the repetitive pattern of fiberglass ceiling tiles passing by, and one of the expressionless paramedics at the end of the gurney whose job it was to move my broken body around. Such is the view often accepted by those knocked down by life: always looking up and feeling low.

My mother and father followed faithfully behind me. My parents tried their best to be stoic. But they couldn't fool me. I knew that they were trying to shut off nightmarish visions of what my life might hold.

Rehab. What a word. It conjures up all sorts of notions. To me it was a place where teams of people stood at the ready to put me back together again exactly like I was before. It never occurred to me that rehabilitation would be far more mental than physical. I remember when the ambulance pulled up outside of the center. There was a man sitting in a wheelchair smoking.

What is this? I thought. *Where am I...some insane asylum?* It was in fact the most lucid place in all of creation. A place of raw reality and of monumental successes and defeats.

All around me people were hobbling about and wheeling around like war wounded. But as I lie there, in a hallway in the rehab, I noticed people in wheelchairs playing pool and going back and forth to the cafeteria. Many were even smiling. I wondered how on earth any of them could be happy. One guy with a gaunt face and stubble on his chin was paralyzed from the neck down. I have no idea who he was but he wore a plaid shirt and was lean, in his forties, and looked like he had once been vital. I remember him sitting there with a long tube dangling out of his mouth. The tube ran all the way down to a cigarette, which was attached to an ashtray resting on the armrest of his wheelchair. Even though I was lying helplessly on a gurney, all I could think was, *What a freak!*

I lay in the hallway for what felt like a long time, my head turned to the side so I could watch the parade of broken bodies scampering past. My father, a big bear of a man with a deep Louisiana drawl, was off demanding that they give me a private room. Apparently the hospital staff didn't care for his approach because before I knew what was happening I was on the move again through a maze of bland white corridors graced only by an occasional print of smiling, happy, wheelchair-bound people. There were nurses and doctors, and the place had the chemical smell of a high school nurse's office.

The man pushing my gurney stopped in the hall outside of a doorway. I caught a glimpse of my parents' faces as he turned me around. My mother was clutching my father's arm and they both wore shallow smiles that failed to cover their distress and concern. After the gurney driver adjusted me so that I wouldn't hit the doorframe, I entered a frightening place. It was as if I had passed through a membrane that brought me into another dimension. From my horizontal view I saw large futuristic-looking machines all over the room. There was a strange smell, like an old folks' home, a place where people aren't bathed everyday. Then I saw them. Mixed up in a mess of tubes and wires and metal were three bodies. They were tethered to the machines like grotesque science experiments, breathing along with the rhythmic rise and fall of artificial lungs. Once I stopped moving and could focus, I realized that I was in a room with three women, all of them paralyzed from the neck down. It did indeed seem like I had entered a world beyond comprehension.

My parents offered polite greetings to the women as they entered. I felt like crying but I bit my lip. I thought frantically, as if some cosmic court was listening to my plea, *How could I, a girl that rarely got into trouble and basically played by the rules, end up in this place?* It didn't seem possible! What was happening to me seemed a horrible punishment that I simply didn't deserve.

My two older sisters, Mitzi and Karen, followed faithfully behind, but I hadn't a clue what was really going on inside their minds. Later Mitzi would tell me that she was flabbergasted and disgusted by what she saw at the hospital. I remember that she complained about the people who surrounded me in the room, saying that they weren't like me. Mitzi resented my mother for being so pragmatic and insisting that they all learn to deal with my injury. My mother alone felt that it was something that wasn't going to go away in a few weeks or months. Mitzi thought that my father had the right idea. Denial! It was a reassuring place to be.

I shared my sister's perspective. It was a matter of self-preservation. We do whatever we have to do in the moment. And so there we were: the family protecting me from their internal squabbles while I hid my fear from everyone, including myself.

My three roommates were all at least ten years older than I. I just couldn't believe their condition. But there they were, simmering inside of themselves. I hated them because it made my situation that much more real. I just didn't want any part of what was happening to me. The rehab, the smells, the women on those machines, the guy smoking a cigarette through a tube...nothing. But I was stuck in a place through a nightmarish sequence of events that continued to get worse by the moment.

The woman on my side of the room had a crazy-looking metal halo apparatus around her head that kept it stabilized on her shoulders. She actually had holes drilled into her head to keep the halo in place. She seemed part human and part machine. After the medics transferred me to my bed and left the room, she said in a pleasant southern twang, "Hi, I'm Karen." Her hair had been butchered by someone and she just generally looked like hell. I wanted to throw up.

In my mind, she had spoken to me like a prisoner greeting a new cell-mate. "Hello, I'm Carlana Stone, pleased to meet you," I responded in my most polite and cheery southern voice, as if I were a visitor and not a patient. *I'm not one of you,* I thought. *So don't talk to me with that "welcome to the club" tone in your voice!* It seemed that no matter how hard I tried, I was at the mercy of people who kept treating me like someone else—like an invalid. I cried a silent scream: *I might not be able to move but I'm no cripple!*

During those first few days, I basically kept to myself, and the center's staff did its best to make me comfortable. In the beginning I was not much better off than the women around me. I wasn't allowed to sit up until I was fitted with a brace, so I spent most of my time lying in bed with white surgical stockings on my legs to prevent swelling. I was at the mercy of others. I could use my arms, but I had to rely on the staff to take care of my basic needs, like the quadriplegics. In the morning and in the evening, someone would come to assist me so that I could go to the bathroom. As a cheerleader and an average seventeen-year-old girl, I was very image-conscious. It was so humiliating, having to rely on a stranger to take away my own waste and clean me. I just wanted to die.

Eating was yet another adventure in biology. I had no appetite and was force-fed through tubes shoved up my nose and down my esophagus. I had been a model patient until the force-feeding. Trust me—it is as awful as it sounds. I remember one nurse, "Cassandra the Giant," who loved me because I was "just the sweetest little thing." Cassandra was a towering brunette who stomped around and had the strength to handle patients who couldn't move themselves. She and I got along just fine until she met my evil twin the day she came at me with those tubes.

Every day Cassandra would roll me around in my bed to fit me for a brace. Every move was filled with shooting pain but I bit my lip and took the agony like a woman. My mother or father or a sister was always on hand. All of us were waiting for the healing to start. We just wanted to get on with it, to start me on the road back to the cheerleading squad and a place in the freshman class at LSU in Baton Rouge.

Love Thy Neighbor, Love Thyself

On the third day, I awoke to the usual routine of feeding and cleaning and I heard a man's voice call into the room from the hallway. In walked a tallish, lanky guy with brown hair and a rosy complexion carrying a little boy who must have been about two years old.

"Hey baby," he called out.

"Oh…hi, hon," Karen, the woman next to me called back. He looked into his little boy's eyes and said in a hushed voice, "Hey Mike, let's go give Mama a big kiss." Then he strode somberly across the room and stood at the head of Karen's bed.

"Mommy," the boy said, looking down at his mother's familiar face.

"Hi, honey, give Mama a kiss." Her husband held their son in such a way that he could reach through the metal apparatus that ringed her head and give his mother a kiss.

"So good to see you sweetie pie." Her arms lay limp and useless by her side, but you could tell from the sound of her voice that she was holding him close and tight someplace in her mind.

Her husband kissed her and whispered, "How you doin'?"

"Okay," she said softly. Her voice was clear and steady. He pulled up a chair and sat down next to her bed for a visit.

That morning, for the first time since my accident, I thought about someone else's fate besides my own. I would've done anything to help that woman hold her little boy.

"Mornin'!" Cassandra called to me in a booming, sunny voice, interrupting my eavesdropping.

"You're gettin' your brace today honey, so you can start sitting up." I broke out of my trance. My brace was arriving, hallelujah! My mom soon entered the room and we told her the good news. Every now and then I would take a momentary break from my tiny victory and look over at Karen and her family.

A few hours later, my excitement turned to horror when the brace was finally delivered. I had envisioned something small and cushiony that would support me and be comfortable to wear. Instead it had the look and feel of a modern-day torture device. I moaned as Cassandra grabbed me with her big mitts and strapped me into the thing. I must have been making a real fuss, because at one point Karen yelled over, "Hey, what're y'all doin' to my neighbor!"

"Torturing me!" I called back.

But Cassandra paid no attention and looked genuinely pleased with herself when she finally fastened the brace. She took a step back, put her hands on her hips, and looked me up and down like a seamstress assessing a new gown. Despite the pain and discomfort, I found myself grateful. It had only been four weeks since the accident but the passage of time seemed like an eternity. Sitting up would be my first step back to normal.

While the brace was a clear indication that this was more serious than we wanted to admit, I think just putting it on gave my mother hope. The smile that brightened my mother's face was the first glimmer of joy I had seen since before the night of the accident. It also drew a clear line between me and the other women in the room. The simple pleasure of regaining a level perspective on the world, especially in the presence of quadriplegics, made me feel blessed. In a small way, the world had begun to right itself.

While my mom might have been the first to realize just how monumental my injury was, she also recognized in that moment that I was going to survive and somehow move forward. That I was going to get better.

Later that afternoon, after my "brace party," my parents decided to go back to the little apartment that they had rented nearby and rest. I bet it was the first night of sound sleep that they'd had in weeks. They left with kisses and the promise of another visit the next day. I could taste my recovery.

Just after my parents left, Karen's husband stood up to leave. Their little boy had conked out on a nearby chair and it was just the two of them. I heard him say, "I love you," which was followed by a very feeble response. He got up, picked up their sleeping child, and brought him over so she could see him. "Goodnight. See you day after tomorrow," he said in a soft voice, so as not to wake the baby. "Yup," was all Karen could say. I was finally sitting up and I tried to keep from looking. But there was no privacy in that room and each of us was privy to the others' most intimate moments. As he walked across the room towards the door, he said goodbye to me and congratulated me on my brace.

"Thanks," I said, with a victorious smile on my face.

After he left I turned to Karen. She lay in exactly the same position as she did when they arrived, as she had lain all day. She made no movements and said nothing. But her eyes offered a glimpse into a world of pain that I had never seen before nor ever experienced since. In those moments after her visit, the agony and tragedy of her fate burned in her eyes.

"Your little boy is just the sweetest thing," I said softly.

"Yes he is," She responded in a quick and deliberate way.

She looked straight ahead and kept her eyes off of me. She wanted to be alone in her pain but was unable to turn away, so I turned away for her. The sun was going down and the room was dimly lit.

I let her rest for some time and then asked her if she wanted something. Not that I could get it myself, but I just couldn't sit there and do nothing. After a while we started to talk about our families and we eventually got to the subject of our accidents. We exchanged our stories. That night, in the midst of all the machines, tubes, and woeful moments, we got to know each other.

She explained that her husband was tortured with guilt because he had been driving her in his truck when its axle broke, unleashing the force that severed her spine below the neck. The car rolled over and her husband walked away unscathed. Karen, however, would never move again. I told her about the Stark Club and my accident. That night I realized that there was a beautiful lady held captive inside that wrecked body, and for the first time since I arrived I didn't feel alone.

Permission and Room to Feel

"God damn it! What the hell is this? They're supposed to be taking care of us. I can't do it myself. This place is a joke! SOMEBODY HELP ME!"

Sandra, or Sandy, was one of the other quadriplegics in room. She was angry at the world and spent her day barking at nurses and screaming at doctors. That was how some of the people in rehab dealt with their pain. They lashed out at everything and everyone. In hindsight, I could have done with some ranting myself. But like a lot of people who experience trauma, I held in all of my feelings and tried to protect everyone from experiencing any pain. Everyone including myself. Avoidance helped me to create and maintain the illusion of control.

"Keep it down, Sandy, I'm comin'," Cassandra said in an exasperated tone as she lumbered into our room.

"Yeah, you're coming while I'm sitting here in my own shit," Sandy barked. Cassandra didn't respond, just put on her mask and gloves and got to work. That woman had the patience of a saint.

Karen and I would look at each other and smile when Sandy would start. It seemed funny to us. The situation was so insane, so out of bounds that you had to laugh or cry. I don't remember when it started, but at a certain point we somehow found comfort in mocking poor old Sandy. Humor is an effective tool in managing stressful situations. Strangely, there was a great deal of humor in the air during those hard days.

"Look at me, I'm Sandra Dee," I would whisper over to Karen when she started up.

"Keep your paws off my silky drawers," Karen would reply in a witty little voice peppered with chuckles.

Meanwhile, the brace that started off as a torture device had become more tolerable. It was like the first piling in a bridge that would eventually reconnect me to my life prior to the accident. I used anything that was associated with a step towards recovery to keep my vision of the future alive. Despite my environment and my own paralysis, when I closed my eyes I could still observe the same strong, beautiful woman that I had always seen staring back at me from my future. She was there smiling and, above all, standing, with a posture that exuded confidence and pride. She comforted me. "This too shall pass," she seemed to say. "You will make it. Come on!" I truly believed that I was different, but reality was stalking me, creeping up on me in physical ways that made it impossible not to accept that I was changing.

After the brace arrived, I began an aggressive regimen of therapy. When I wasn't lying in my bed chatting with Karen or making fun of Sandra, I was involved in a variety of tasks designed to make me strong and independent.

Behavioral Medicine

My morning started with an intimate encounter with Big Cassandra. It is really hard to comprehend sudden paralysis. One moment you're moving about, in control of your most basic needs, and the next you're totally at the mercy of others. It is a humbling reality. She helped me take care of my bodily functions in as dignified a manner as possible. After we finished, she would heave me up like a sack of potatoes and transfer me to a wheelchair so an orderly could take me to the behavioral doctor's office. It was nice to get out of the room. To me it was just another baby step towards freedom. First the hallways, then the parking lot, and then presto—senior year and off to school.

Maka Merritt was a cute little brunette who served as the behavioral medicine doctor on staff. In non-medical terms, she was a shrink. Every other day, I was wheeled down to her little office, teetering around in my brace like a turtle sitting up in her shell. When you're in denial there is nothing more annoying than someone wanting you to talk about things like feelings and fears. At first I pooh-poohed her attempt to help me because I just didn't understand why I had talk about anything given that I was going to be walking again soon. But in time I was able to get past some of my resentfulness and really talk to her. She had a very calm way about her. She would turn towards her door when they wheeled me in and say, "How we doin?"

"Fine, just fine," I used to respond, as if the situation couldn't be more normal, my back stiff as a scarecrow's due to the brace, and the memory of Cassandra helping me clean myself fresh in my mind.

"So what's been going on?" she would ask in her soft and intimate way.

I have to say that this was one of the most important elements of my rehab experience, having someone unrelated to my life prior to the accident ask me basic questions about myself. As I've suggested, after a trauma we often try to run from reality and construct a false worldview in which to hide. For me it was a matter of self preservation and a desire to protect my family from hurt. However, in doing so, I created the proverbial situation of no one wanting to address the elephant in the room. Maka helped me start to acknowledge the beast.

I told her about a strange recurring dream that I was having about Karen, my roommate. In my dream, someone would be shooting at her. I would run in and carry her out of the line of fire to safety. It just kept happening. I talked; Maka listened. I told her about my family and the accident and how hard it was. Our typical conversation went something like this: "I just feel so bad," I'd say. "It hurts me so much to see their faces and put them through this."

"I know it does," was all she would say.

She listened without judgment and spoke in a way that made it seem like whatever I was feeling was okay. She just gave me space to feel. I think that anyone who is dealing with a sudden change needs, more than anything else, someone to help them by simply giving them permission and room to be in touch with their emotions.

I would tell her how it was going to be. That I would over-come my injury and walk into my future to claim my proper and rightful destiny: to become the woman that I was raised to be.

"I just want this to be over. I mean, I am not going to be this way for long," I'd tell her in an exasperated tone. "Have you seen that boy who walks around with a foot brace? He's got the same kind of injury as me and he's just doing fine. If he can do it, I can do it! I'm a gymnast and a cheerleader. This is no big task—not for me! Forget it! I just want to spare everyone from any of this. I mean, *I* can handle it, I just can't stand seeing how much pain this whole thing is causing *them*."

Maka just listened. She would look at me with the steady gaze of a professional therapist and neither challenge nor encourage my vision. Her neutrality drove me nuts and made me feel like I had to convince her that my version of the future would come to pass. Somehow, I believed that the more people bought into my version of the future, the more I would ensure its coming to pass.

A little bell would chime, and I would know that my time with Maka was over for the day. A knock on the door would announce the arrival of the orderly who had come to wheel me down to respiratory therapy. The people down there were the polar opposite of Maka's dignified calm.

Learning to Breathe

Recovery from trauma is laden with trap doors and illusions. Just when you think you've turned a corner, that you are on your way to being healed, something will occur to remind you that all is not well. Respiratory therapy revealed certain truths about my condition that I didn't want to see, as well as truths about how to handle people whose identity was under siege.

Walking into the respiratory therapy room was like walking into Mr. Roger's living room. Twisters could be touching down in the parking lot, but Darlene, the annoying therapist in charge, would always greet me with, "Well good mornin' Carlana. C'mon in, sunshine!"

Darlene had big blonde hair, a rather gawky body and wore bright blue eye shadow. God, how I wanted to just smack that woman.

Respiratory therapy was the ultimate slap in the face for me. In my mind, it was reserved for the truly far gone, for the quadriplegics—who in the rehab were known simply as "The Quads." And therefore why I, the once and future athlete, had to participate was beyond me.

"How we doin' today? We have a spot for you right over here. Got it all ready for you," she'd say. She was just way too perky for someone dealing with people new to wheelchairs and body braces!

Before I'd start my exercises, Darlene would lean in closely and offer words of encouragement, "Carlana, I know you can do this; now let's give it your best shot this time." Then she would have me blow into a tube that was connected to a clear plastic container containing little white balls. My challenge was to try to make the balls float to the top of the chamber.

She and her silly cronies would sit there screaming like cheerleaders on the sidelines. "C'mon Carlana! You can do it!" Can you imagine the pathetic scene? Grown women cheering other grown women to blow plastic balls in the air. I wanted to scream, "Shut the hell up! It's a stinking ball and a piece of plastic. And you don't look like cheerleaders! Leave that to me. I'm the damn cheerleader here!" There is nothing worse than patronizing sentiment when you are dealing with grim realities, no matter how well intentioned.

And then there was the pain that would shoot down my spine whenever I blew into the contraption. This slap of reality stung me to the core. It made me wonder if I would ever feel normal again. Just when I would start to feel a little better, it would remind me that something was really wrong with me. It was amazing that something as simple as breathing could be painful. Day by day, I could feel my identity slowly slipping away.

No Way Back

"Get it out, it's clogged. Hurry, she can't breathe!" the nurse screamed. "Hold on Karen, we're almost done."

"Ready, look out," one nurse told the other as she wound up and slammed her hand against Karen's little chest. "One more time." She struck her so hard that I heard the thud as her hand made contact with Karen's rib cage. The other nurse stood above Karen shoving a tube down her throat, sucking out the phlegm and mucus that had clogged her airway. It always seemed to happen at night when the room was dark, except for the light around Karen's bed.

After it was all over, I'd just sit there praying and hoping, self-ishly, to get out of that room as soon as I could. It was just too hard to see that kind of suffering when there was no end in sight.

By now, my own breathing had improved to the point that I could start physical therapy. Susan Krall was my therapist. Suzie, as I called her, was adorable. We bonded immediately. She would stretch my legs and try to isolate the muscles that were functioning. She used to hold my leg in a particular position and ask me to move, but all I could do was struggle and struggle and that leg would not move. *These damn legs!* I would silently curse.

One day a doctor came into the therapy room and performed a kind of sensitivity test on me. He took a needle and began to prick my legs. "Tell me when you stop feeling it," he said.

He started at my waist, pricking me where my sensation was normal, and moved down. After he got past my upper thigh, I couldn't sense a thing. This was my first real moment of panic since the accident. I remember looking at him sticking that sharp pin in my leg and wondering why I couldn't feel it. I refused to accept what was happening to me. To me! *What have I done to deserve this? And when will I be* normal *again?* I thought in a panic. Suzie and the doctor looked at each other in silence. I was afraid to ask what was going through their heads.

That afternoon I was wheeled back into my room. I was scared. I suppose I was very quiet, which is definitely not like me. By now, Karen knew my personality and could sense that something was up.

"You okay?" she asked.

"Some man just did a kind of test on me," I said. "He took a pin and he pricked me down my legs."

"Did it hurt?" she asked.

"I couldn't feel it," I said, in a frustrated exhale. Now it was me who couldn't bring my eyes up to meet hers.

"Oh, well it's still early, honey," Karen responded.

"Yea, I know, but they didn't seem very hopeful."

"What did they say?"

"They didn't say anything," I said looking at her. "They didn't say a damn thing."

"Carlana, you're going to be okay, no matter what happens." She said it with a smile on her face, lying flat on her back, unable to move a muscle, in the same position she had been in for weeks. "You are so special, I know you'll be fine. I just know." The breathing machine rose and fell. The setting sun filled the room, and so it was, the quadriplegic comforting the cheerleader.

Not long after that day I was fitted for a wheelchair: the product of that silent moment between Suzie and the doctor.

A wheelchair? I thought, *Why do I need a wheelchair specifically designed and fitted for me? That's ridiculous! I'll just use this big ole hospital clunker until I'm able to get back on my feet.* But they had been through this drill with hundreds of others and they knew...they just knew. The unbearable had quickly become the new normal.

Marooned on the Crippling Plains of Doubt

The staff at the rehab was thrilled with my progress. According to them, I was healing beautifully. And true, I was able to move about under my own power, wheeling down hallways and getting into and out of my wheelchair. But I was nowhere near the place that I considered healed. I was still sitting down and I had not moved a single muscle in my legs since the accident.

I finally got to the point where I was able to leave the rehab for lunch with my parents. I remember going outside and breathing the fresh air for the first time since my arrival. The sun felt strong against my pale skin. I inhaled deeply and savored the fragrant scent of earth and plants that hung in the dry Texas air. The scent made me want to get up and run through the grass. And just then those heavy words that the doctor told me, "You may never walk again," came flooding into my consciousness and cemented me to my chair.

My father pulled the car around and, thanks to the rigorous training at the rehab, I had developed a method for getting into and out of cars by myself. I had a long board that I would place under my butt while sitting in my wheelchair that ran to the back seat of the car. I would lift myself up and slowly inch my way across the board and into the car. The technique worked beautifully in rehab and I really looked forward to a great lunch out with my parents.

We pulled up to the restaurant somewhere outside of Dallas. It was fairly large and there was a valet stand positioned just outside of an awning that stretched from the door. My father parked the car and the valet came over to his door to give him a claim ticket and take the keys. I turned to my right, and standing under the awning was a party of four waiting for their car. The valet took my father's keys and my father told him, "Just one minute please."

He got up, walked to the trunk, opened it, and pulled out my collapsible wheelchair and the board. He went over to my side of the car, the side facing the waiting people, and opened my door. Another party had joined the one already waiting and they were watching my father put the wheelchair together. He put one end of the board on the chair and the other next to me on the back seat. He held the chair steady and I began to make my way across it. The crowd stared unabashedly at the small drama unfolding before them. I kept my eyes on the board and away from them.

I tried to keep focused and in my mind I ran through the process as if it was a gymnastics event. Lift...steady...legs together...move...down. Lift...legs together...move...down. I repeated the process until I was about halfway across the board. At that moment I looked up at the crowd. It was just a split second, but it was long enough for me to see the emotion on their faces. Staring back at me were not the harsh eyes of malice or open faces of admiration. These were all things I had encountered in school or at gymnastics competitions. The crowd had cast something foreign and unsettling upon me. For the first time in my life, I, the champion athlete, had engendered pity.

My father could sense my unease and he rushed me into the restaurant as quickly as possible. I just stared at the ground and avoided eye contact with all of them as we passed by. Those people and their unwavering stares triggered huge pangs of doubt in my heart. I can't remember the meal that followed or anything that happened after that. But the memory of getting out of the car, completely debilitated and with all those people staring, still haunts me. To this day I hate using a valet. I'd rather park my car myself and wheel for a mile than be the focus of such sorrowful sentiment. Nothing is worth that kind of humiliation.

This would become my biggest struggle, fighting off looks of pity. It is sometimes hard to keep people focused on you and not on your disability when it is obvious like mine. Whether you are like me and have a visible disability or your disability is on the inside, when the world knows your story and assumes your grief, it is an effort to work your way through the veil of their perception.

That night I returned to the rehab feeling the lowest that I had yet felt. I slipped into my bed and just stared quietly at the ceiling. I tried desperately to call upon the proud woman that I had seen in my future. I longed for her smile, but she was starting to fade and I struggled to find something that would breathe life into her once more. But everywhere I looked there were signs of deep-rooted change. My legs were thinning. My butt, once solid as a rock, was starting to lose its form. I remember lying there, wondering what was happening to me. What was happening to the parts of me that had been so central to my being? I was literally coming apart and my identity was slipping away right in front of my eyes. There was nothing that I could do to stop it. I rolled over and fell into a dreamless sleep.

I awoke later that night to a dark room, silent except for the rhythmic sound of breathing machines. I looked across the room at all the tubes and medical devices. I asked myself a frightening question, *What is going to become of me?* I needed a sign, something to give me hope and help me understand how to deal with what was happening. I closed my eyes and saw a barren landscape where there was once bounty. All the life events that hung so vividly before me just three months earlier were left in tatters. My dreams and goals had all lost their form. But most striking of all was the change in the strong woman, my future self, the North Star that I had grown to love. Gone was the smile that inspired me. She no longer stood proudly before me.

"What happened?" a soft voice called to me out of the darkness. I turned towards Karen and then back again.

"Nothing," I responded.

"What happened," Karen said again.

I didn't know how to respond. How could I tell her about my worries and fears? She, a mother who would never hold her little boy again. How could I tell such a person about my doubt?

"We went to the restaurant today. It was awful. Everyone stared at me. Everyone just looked at me with pity. It was actually painful. I must look pretty bad, because they just made me feel like a...like a cripple."

"People don't mean it. They don't know what to do."

"So they just stare."

"Yes, so they just stare. They can't believe that life could be so unfair. And they let themselves imagine, just for a second, how it would feel if it was them. It's nothing, but it's enough for them to feel horror and pity. I see it in my husband's face. I see it in everyone's face."

For a while I didn't respond. We just lay there, two people fending off the fear, feeling helpless and insignificant.

"Three months ago I was a gymnast. I was president of the class. I did things and made a difference. What can I do now? I can barely take care of myself. Just getting out of a car requires this stupid exercise. I mean, what am I supposed to do?"

"You can do nothing more than what you're doing. Three months ago, when you came here, you couldn't even go to the bathroom by yourself. Look at you now. You don't know what's going to happen. But in the meantime, you just keep going. I see you and I know your victories will be many, Carlana."

The street lamp outside cast a soft glow in our room, its bluish light streaming in through the slats in the blinds.

"Why are you up?" I asked her.

"It's my arms; they're hurting." Karen's arms sometimes ached because of the lack of circulation.

I looked over at her. There she was, as she always had been. Lying down, facing the ceiling, her arms by her sides. Your victories will be many. I mulled it over. And then I thought about my dream and saving her from the bullets. I looked over at her little body and white arms that appeared almost blue in the soft light. Sitting up, I reached over and positioned my wheelchair below the side of the bed. A feeling of determination pulsed through me. It was as if I was on the balance beam once more. I placed one hand on the chair and the other on the bed and readied for my dismount. *Lift*, I thought, raising my body off of the bed and transferring it in one graceful motion to the chair below. I placed my feet into the foot rest and wheeled across to Karen.

I sat before her. Her breathing machine rose and fell. Her left arm lay before me at eye level.

"What are you doin'?" She asked.

I reached up and placed my hands on her arm and started softly massaging her. I began at her bicep and worked my way down to her swollen red fingers. Karen's arms were so soft and white. They were covered with short blond hairs that were as fine as a baby's. With a deliberate touch, I rubbed her atrophied arm as if it were speaking to me, telling me where and how to touch her.

"How's this." I asked.

"Good."

After about ten minutes I rolled around to the other side and worked on her other arm. She sighed and kept thanking me as I worked on her. Another ten minutes passed and I rolled across the room and lifted myself into my bed.

"Carlana?"

"Yes?"

"Thank you."

"You're welcome."

"No, I mean...thank you. Thank you so much."

"You're so welcome sweetie. Thank you."

I laid back and closed my eyes. I thought about how sometimes the smallest victories will give you amazing strength. Easing Karen Jordan's pain was a powerful experience. Suddenly

I saw potential and hope where just hours before were uncertainty and bleakness. A bright optimistic dawn filled my life's horizon. The landscape was new and clean and waiting to be explored. But most importantly, my muse, my innermost self, sat smiling back at me with pride and certainty. She was still beautiful and confident and her smile offered a benediction that told me that, no matter what happened, the same qualities that made me a champion and a leader were still inside of me.

I looked at Karen for a moment. She lay peacefully in her bed, eyes closed, drifting off to sleep. I too closed my eyes and once again drifted off to sleep, confident with the knowledge that I could still make a difference.

Lesson Learned: *The Indestructible You*

At seventeen, or maybe at any age, it's hard to think in terms of forever, hard to imagine that a single event can leave a permanent, indelible imprint on your life. I certainly couldn't and didn't want to. But when we finally begin to take in our "new normal," we begin the process of reconciling our reality with the projection we have of ourselves. What we get is a benediction from the former self to the new. A sign that despite how hurt we might be, inside or out, we are still, at our core, the same person we always were.

All of us will most likely experience a dramatic life challenge. It may be physical or mental. The breakup of a marriage or the loss of a child might trigger the same feelings of uncertainty that I experienced. Even the natural act of aging might place us in an alien and unfamiliar place.

No matter what your life challenge is or will be, you must try to remember that nothing can really shake the foundations of who you really are. These things are like the elements; there is nothing that can destroy or break them. You, in your own way, are a perfect creation, and you will surface again.

Asking Why

That is not to say that there will not be moments of uncertainty and doubt. But try to use these moments to ask yourself why you are feeling fear. During my time in rehab and after, I tried to understand what was happening and what it meant for my future. I had to understand how all the changes I experienced were going to impact my life, and how or if I could manage them. I was afraid. But in time I learned why I was afraid, and through that process discovered a great deal about my self.

I learned that my fear was tied to specific notions of my identity. I had always felt in control of my destiny and made a difference in the lives of people around me. I had been a leader. I had been physically active and attractive. I feared that my injury, my life challenge, had taken those qualities and the opportunities they presented away from me. But then I learned that this was impossible. The simple act of rubbing Karen Jordan's arms revealed this truth.

Karen Jordan was a friend and nurturer to me at a time when I tried to keep my pain from my family and friends. Karen was someone with whom I could share my hurt: someone who understood exactly what I was going through.

More than that, she was an example of how it is possible to suffer a seemingly unendurable loss without growing bitter.

While the other women in the room lashed out at the world, she displayed courage and grace. Helping her was a way for me to honor her friendship and support and showed me a new way to measure the value of my actions. It made me realize that a gift from the heart carries the same value regardless of its size.

It is critical that we allow ourselves to explore our fears because at the root of them are key notions of our own identities. You will most likely find that your fear of not being able to realize your goals and dreams is based in your belief that you have lost a piece of your self, your core, forever. I find that this is often because we judge ourselves from the outside in, from how the world will perceive or interpret us. When you are challenged, it is time to begin taking the world to task and start acting from the inside out in the most honest of ways.

In these early days of my journey I learned a wonderful truth: YOU ARE INDESTRUCTIBLE.

Living Proof: *Remembering One's Self-Worth*

When I began talking to people about my experiences, I remember meeting a special person who opened up to me and took my message to heart. Her name was Barbara.

Barbara had experienced a sudden and devastating life event. She was thirty-three and about to purchase a home with her husband of five years. They had begun planning for a baby and she was looking forward to raising a family. She was, in fact, realizing the life-long dream that so many women share: having a committed, loving relationship and experiencing the joys of motherhood. Her entire identity was wrapped up in the life that she had built with her husband. Everything seemed on schedule.

One day Barbara met her husband in front of their house on his way home from work. She greeted him with a smile but she received a grave and alien stare that, even at that early moment she says, told her that her world was about to come undone. "What's wrong?" she pleaded. After a moment of silence, he looked her in the eye and told her that he was leaving her. He informed her that their marriage was over: he did not want to buy a home, have a child, or build a life with her. And then he literally left. In ten minutes he stripped her of her identity and left her alone to ponder what she had done do drive him away.

Her eyes welled up with tears as she described her fear that she might never resurface from the layers of shame and disappointment that the event piled on top of her. She had always perceived herself as a loving, attractive, and intelligent person who was worthy of all the joys that come with sharing oneself and building a fulfilling future with someone special. After the shock of abandonment had begun to wear off, Barbara questioned her very identity and found herself asking many of the same questions I had asked myself in rehab: "What good am I now?"; "How can anybody ever love me again?" My heart broke for her.

Together we examined her experience. She had lost her husband, her home, and the possibility of a family. She felt like she had lost everything. I wanted her to feel that all was not lost. Taking her hands in mine, I gently reminded her that she was the same strong and attractive woman that she had been before her husband left her. I remembered back to when I was young and I used to attend Serendipity workshops with my father. They were, in essence, personal growth seminars. It was there that I learned a lot of exercises I could do to get in touch with myself and my feelings. I remembered one exercise specifically that I thought might help Barbara.

The exercise demonstrates the power of the spoken word. Barbara feared that when her husband left her she was permanently damaged, that a part of her had disappeared with him.

I asked Barbara to really focus on herself. What did she have to contribute to the world? What good was she, really? I had her list the qualities she valued and repeat them over and over again. She said things like, "I am a good friend. I am a good daughter." We had hit on something there. Barbara began to reflect on what a wonderful asset she had been to her mother. She had stayed with her after Barbara's father died and she had helped her to continue living. I could see a glimmer of hope come back to Barbara's eyes. It was a small acknowledgement but it was something positive in an otherwise bleak landscape.

Slowly she started to recognize the good things she had left in her life. The things that no one could ever take from her. I suggested that she might use those same skills to become a wonderful mother one day and it offered her hope. She began to feel worthy of happiness again and set out to live the next day feeling a little bit better about herself.

The exercise didn't fix Barbara's problem but it did enable her to take a step back and be a little more objective about what she had to offer the world. Sometimes small victories are all we have to keep us going.

It took commitment and hard work but Barbara finally made it back. She joined a group and relied on friends to help her through dark moments and eventually learned to believe in herself once more. She recognized her gifts and what she has to offer the world around her. And that's when she began to let others back into her life.

Today, she is married and a mom. She is pregnant with her second child and is living the life she's always dreamed of. Barbara's life proves that even when precious attributes are stripped away from us we can rely on our fundamental strengths to carry us through. She is proof that we are indestructible.

· EXERCISES ·

Create a collage of things you love about yourself

For this you will need several magazines, a large sheet of paper, tape or glue, and some scissors. Sort through the magazine and cut out words, phrases, and pictures which describe you and the things you like about yourself.

Hang the collage in a place you frequent everyday (next to your computer at work or by the bathroom mirror). Make a point to recognize and celebrate these positive things and you will undoubtedly feel better about yourself. When we focus on the good things instead of the bad, we realize our gifts and know that we are indestructible regardless of what might be going on in our lives at the present time.

And as you feel more positive about yourself, you may want to add new things to your collage.

Count your blessings

Record, on a daily basis, two to three things for which you are grateful. For example, you might write about a child giving you a hug, a spouse saying, "I love you," or receiving a letter from an old friend. If you do these things, it has been scientifically proven that you will experience greater optimism, connectedness to others, and even more peaceful sleep.

Try this exercise three days a week for two months. Your outlook on life will be more positive and your confidence in yourself will grow.

CHAPTER 3

Masking the Pain

A Sense of Otherness

The Colorado sun shone brightly the day our car crested the hill overlooking the town of Boulder. There before us was the front range of the Rocky Mountains, stretching to the north and south as far as the eye could see. Just beyond the town, the dark Flatiron rocks dangled above the red tiled roofs of the University of Colorado like a giant mobile. It was a majestic sight and, for the first time since leaving Shreveport, a smile crept across my face as I imagined spending the next four years in such an inspiring place.

We sped down the hill towards the town and campus below us and slowly signs of college life started to emerge from the palate of red roofs and earth-colored buildings. Towards the end of town stood two giant dorms called Williamsburg. As we passed the buildings, I could see students, young eighteen-year-olds like me, unpacking cars and carrying mundane items designed to serve domestic needs: soup warmers, fans, and mini refrigerators seemed to be popular accoutrements of college life. But rather than excitement at the prospect of meeting new people and the sheer joy of being able to explore such a wonderful place, the sight of those students, all healthy and vivacious, their strong legs exposed in the late summer sun, sent a bolt of anxiety into the pit of my stomach that stole the joy from the idealistic setting.

Since the accident, powerful waves of uncertainty and doubt periodically rattled my self-confidence. Just when I thought I had a grip on things, when I felt I could manage my situation and could deal with the world, I would be whipped back into the scary landscape that I thought I had left behind in rehab. As I rolled into Boulder that morning, seeing all those young bodies, I feared that no one would ever embrace me, a girl in a wheelchair.

My mom drove the car towards the center of town. Boulder really was beautiful; a hive of youthful exuberance, brimming with young, good-looking kids. I saw flashes of my former self here and there in pretty girls crossing the street or running in sweats to some practice or event. I saw Dead Heads mingling with preppies as they walked to and from the shops on The Hill, the small neighborhood just to the west of the campus. There was a general carefree feel to the place and a hip mixture of groovy 60s' psychedelic anti-fashion and 80s' Polo chic. Think Haight-Ashbury meets Ralph Lauren. But there was one object that was notably absent from the landscape: I didn't see one wheelchair. And in a flash I had a strong sense of my otherness.

A good-looking couple came out of a bookstore walking arm in arm. As we drove past, the boy made eye contact with me. His gaze lingered for a moment and then he looked away, wrapping his arm around his girlfriend. The way he held her reminded me of James, my old boyfriend.

What have I done to myself? I pondered nervously. But what came out of my mouth was, "Isn't this cool!" With a quick look to the left, I smiled for my mom and momentarily banished my insecurity.

"It sure is," my mom said in her soft, kind voice. She looked at me for just a second as if to make sure that I was really as excited as I seemed. Mothers have a way of knowing what's really going on with their kids. She accepted my enthusiasm as genuine, even if just for my sake, and tried to enjoy the ritual act of dropping her youngest daughter off at college, to reconnect with the timeline of normality. And as we drove through the town with its perfect streets and perfect people, I had an overwhelming desire to conceal the damaged part of myself from the seemingly unflawed world around me.

The last thing I wanted was for people to see me as helpless. I just couldn't stomach the idea of people looking at me with pity, as "the poor little girl in the wheelchair." The memory of my first public outing as a paraplegic and the moment when I felt the sting of pity was still fresh in my mind. Pity, to me, was just another form of rejection, because it meant that people would not be able to see me for what I was: a young, vibrant woman full of life and potential. In my desire to conceal, to fit in, I summoned all my strengths and charged ahead.

See No Pain—Feel No Pain

In Japan there is form of puppet-theater called Bunraku. In Bunraku, puppeteers dressed completely in black share the stage with their anthropomorphic miniatures, projecting into them the personalities of warriors and other storied characters from Japanese lore. All the puppeteers are covered from head to toe in black cloth except for the master puppeteer, who is allowed to share the stage with his diminutive protagonist without a face mask. The master is so complete in his possession of the inanimate body that he fades into the infinite darkness of the black stage until the audience only sees the brilliant character, which, wielding a sword or tumbling through the air, in a reenactment of some ancient battle scene, seems blessed with superhuman powers. Like the master puppeteer, cloaked behind the dynamic personality that he projects into his marionette, I found myself only showing the world the parts of me that compensated for my physical weaknesses so that I could blend into my surroundings.

I had always been strong and upbeat. The Carlana that the world had known and loved before the accident was a bubbly super-achiever. Whether I was struggling to stay on the balance beam to carry myself and my team to victory, making an empowering speech as class president or simply enjoying the attention of boys, my tenacity and positive attitude were always my best qualities. Being the fighter, the leader, and the sex object was my natural state, and it was one that I would try to maintain in an effort to be accepted and ultimately loved by my peers.

Despite my tenacity, I wasn't the same person that I had been before the accident, physically or emotionally. My essence was the same. The most important parts of me were intact, but I had, in some very pragmatic and complex ways, been altered. In the process of managing my situation, I hid the part of myself that felt the pain, the very human and vulnerable girl with wants and needs just like any other. Like a master puppeteer, I hoped to eclipse the chair with my positive energy and would show no moments of weakness or suffering, for my own benefit and for that of others around me. I banished any negative feelings that welled up inside of me back down into the subconscious from which they rose, holding them at bay until I reached a place where I would be able to hear above the din of my woes.

Wheelchair...what wheelchair? I said to myself. I would be bubbly and cute and excited about everyone and everything around me. I believed that if I acted like an individual who had utter control over her life and destiny, it would be so. I strove to be the quintessential un-victim.

The thing is...it worked, at least initially. People only saw what I wanted them to see. They ate me up and thought I was just the happiest person alive. Later I would be told that I had inspired many by my single-mindedness and positive energy. I was so successful with my strategy that no one ever dreamed I was overcompensating and trying to overcome huge insecurities. I successfully hid the proverbial elephant in the room. For a time I even hid him from myself.

My mom and I drove around the campus and pulled up in front of a beige brick building called Libby Hall. Once again I was moving into some kind of institution. I had a flashback to the day I arrived at rehab and was pushed helplessly on a gurney down long sterile hallways. But the difference between the hospital and Libby Hall was profound. I was fully mobile now and armed with a high-tech wheelchair that I could maneuver with ease. I entered Libby with as much pride and confidence as I could muster and rolled on through those halls as if the chair was my preferred mode of transportation.

Besides the fact that I was in more control, Libby Hall differed from the rehab in the way that an elementary school differs from a nursing home. It was full of life and color and you could feel a sense of youth and vitality about the place. Libby Hall was part of a beginning rather than an end, and the energy the college dorm exuded was infectious.

Talking Over My Disability

All the dorm-room doors had two construction-paper signs on them, each bearing one of the two residents' names. There were Janet and Stephanie and Gina and Margaret. And then there was my door. It had just one name written on a kidney-shaped piece of light blue construction paper. Carlana Stone, it had originally read. But someone had already added an apostrophe S and a D to the sign so it read "Carlana's Stoned." My mom just smirked and raised her eyebrows. This was the University of Colorado at Boulder after all, though we honestly had no idea of its fame for being the biggest party school in the country. Remember, I was supposed to go to Louisiana State University in Baton Rouge but switched to Boulder at the last minute in order to be closer to a top-notch rehab center for spinal cord injuries in Denver. Soon after my arrival in Colorado, however, the center would determine that my injury was beyond the scope of their treatments and I would be denied the hope of a cure in the short-term. But ultimately, Boulder would become a place of healing for me.

In Libby, I had a private room while most all of the other students in the dorm had to share rooms with one another. It was borne out of a perceived need for more space and privacy. In hindsight, it was just another way that I was able to keep people from seeing the real me: from seeing anything that I felt would be ugly or embarrassing and cause people to reject me, just as I felt James had done after the accident.

My mom helped me settle into the room. After we brought in all of my bags, we moved my two single beds together to form one big bed and she left to check in to her hotel. As I put my things away, paranoia crept in and I found myself wondering if I would become a landmark of sorts for the kids in the dorm. That kids might use me when trying to explain themselves. Not in a malicious way mind you, but simply to ensure comprehension:

> *"It's on the first floor."*
> *"You mean on the hall with that girl in the wheelchair?"*
> *"No, no, the other one."*
> *"Oh, okay."*

As I contemplated my fate in this new place, there was a knock on the door. I looked up expecting to see one of the cute freshman girls from down the hall stopping in to say hello. Instead I found a good looking, tan, slightly foppish boy standing in my doorway with a broad smile on his face. Even just standing, he had a kind of outgoing social presence that I identified with and I instantly liked him. Beside him was a fresh-faced girl with long brown hair. She was cute but didn't hold a candle to the dandy standing next to her. Fate, my recent foe, had decided to serve up something wonderful.

"Hi, we're just making the rounds, sizing things up if you will," he said in a slightly erudite manner, a bit out of line for his age. I could tell that this boy came from something or somewhere special, or at least he thought he did. Either way, I liked his energy.

"Well come on in," I instantly replied.

"I'm Tucker Hitchcock and this is BG," he said motioning to the girl beside him, quickly stepping in front of her and walking into the room.

"Hi," she added in a sweet little voice.

"Nice to meet you. I'm Carlana!"

Did he say Hitchcock? Well that explains a lot, I thought. But this utterance, neither confirming nor denying relation to an American icon, would eventually come back to haunt him. They walked into my room, which Tucker scanned like an assessor. He was, indeed, sizing me up. I guess my brand-name clothes combined with the fact that I had a single room must have met his standards because he immediately sat down on my bed and made himself comfortable. Even at that early moment I think we both sensed some kind of common ground and knew that we would become close friends.

"Where y'all from?" he said, imitating my southern drawl.

"Shreveport, Louisiana," I said, feigning a tone of offense in my voice. "How bout y'all?"

"I'm from Palm Beach and BG's from Seattle," he said.

"Wow...Seattle!" I responded enthusiastically, just to irk him.

We chatted a bit, they on the bed and I in my wheelchair. He was totally unimpressed with the chair and before I knew it he'd lit a cigarette and offered me one. Of course I accepted though, at the time, I didn't smoke.

"So is it true?" he said, taking a drag of his cigarette and pointing towards the door.

"Is what true?" I said looking around.

"Are you *stoned*? Better yet, do you have any?" he said with a smile, but I could tell that he was serious.

"No, unfortunately not, I don't smoke. Well, pot anyway," I said in kind of a whisper, looking at my cigarette.

"Not yet anyway," he said, taking a drag from his cigarette and scanning the room once more to see if he had missed anything of interest.

I'm not sure how it happened but within about twenty minutes I found myself planning a margarita party that was to be held in my room later that night. Sitting in my room with Mr. Palm Beach and company made a party seem like an obvious way to get things started. And besides, it would fit my strategy of distraction through relentless positive motion. People would see how cool I was and that I wasn't just some invalid.

BG left us and Tucker and I walked the halls introducing ourselves to all the young women, inviting them to the party later that night. Everyone was into it and I felt like my old self again: charismatic, in control, and leading. But in reality, a desperate need for validation was being satisfied deep inside of me. I operated under the conviction that if I could just win these people over, if I could be embraced and treated like BG or any other girl in my dorm, I would feel whole again.

I worked that dorm like a Scarlet O'Hara planning a party at Tara Hall.

"Hi, how y'all doin? I'm Carlana, this is Tucker, and we're havin' a margarita party later on. Come on over." With each new doorway, my voice got louder and louder as if I was trying to speak over my disability.

After visiting about ten rooms, we approached a room that had the names Gina and Tammy on the outside. The door was slightly ajar so we knocked. "Anybody home?" I inquired.

"Come on in," a voice called back.

We pushed the door open and inside, sitting on the floor with her feet pointed towards us, wearing nothing but the shortest of shorts, was a pretty girl with long brown hair moisturizing her legs. Not just any legs, but long, tan, powerful gams that looked like they belonged on a Rockette!

"Hi!" she said smiling, still paying more attention to her legs than she did to us. She had this "yes, come on in and behold the glory, I know you want to" manner about her. Or at least it seemed so to me. Tucker's eyes were popping out of his head. He was attracted to pretty girls in the same way that a designer drools over a hot new model. To him, they were tools of validation.

She was confident and perky and I could tell that she had been popular in high school. But those legs, they seemed to stretch for miles in front of her. I had goose bumps. I had chills. This girl was me before my accident! I looked down for an instant at my own skinny limbs and thought, *Oh my God! What's happened to me! Don't just sit there, do something!* On her dresser was a picture of a good-looking guy with longish brown hair. I don't know if it was just the moment or if there was an actual resemblance, but for the second time that day I was reminded of James, and how, save for one unfortunate night in Texas, I could be that beautiful girl sitting on the floor, lavishing her powerful legs with love and attention. I hated those legs—hers and mine.

"I'm Tucker and this is Carlana and we're having a party later on at about seven. Why don't you drop by?" She was obviously a member of an A-list social scene and that was exactly the kind of person that he liked to surround himself with: people that were young, attractive, popular, and with an air of entitlement.

"Party...?" she said questioningly as if pondering the meaning of the word.

"Margarita party," I said, helping her out.

"Margarita? Yum! I'm Gina."

"Where ya from Gina?" Tucker queried.

"Huntington Beach. How 'bout you?"

"Palm Beach," Tucker immediately spat back.

"Louisiana," I said.

"Oooh...New Orleans?" she asked, momentarily looking up from her legs.

"No, Shreveport."

"Oh, I don't know it," she replied.

"It's up north. Anyway, you definitely have to come by tonight."

"I will!" she said in an overly enthusiastic way.

And with that I bid her goodbye and dragged Tucker out of the room and towards the next door, doing my best to recover from Gina and her legs. To my relief it contained a rather plain-Jane type. Tucker barely even acknowledged her.

I felt confident that first day and, except for my encounter with Gina, even forgot about the wheelchair. But after I was alone in my room, I felt doubtful about the evening. I just didn't know if I could rely on these kids to see beyond the chair and embrace me. Young people are just not used to hanging out with girls in wheelchairs and I feared that I might have made a big mistake in assuming they would want to hang out with me. In my mind, I could hear them asking each other, *"Are you going to go to that girl's room, you know, the one in the wheelchair?"* And I could see their faces as they sneered and shook their heads to say no. I thought I might be sitting there alone with my new friend Tucker.

Apparently, word got out around the dorm that there was a huge bash on the first floor and by seven there were about thirty people sitting around my room, drinking margaritas, smoking cigarettes, and having a blast. I was at the center of everything and everyone. It felt great. It was just like the good ole days back in Shreveport. Tucker, in his khaki shorts, topsiders, and Izod shirt, was yapping away with every pretty girl in the room. Every now and then he would disappear and return more bubbly than ever, talking in the carefree way that comes from a life of extreme privilege. As for me, I was doing my best to be a bigger and louder partier than anyone else. Distract and conquer.

The party was important for me. I was looking, of course, for the kind of acceptance that comes from winning the approval of others, the same kind of validation that goes along with being popular. I was very young and it would be some time before I realized that true strength, strength that is unshakable, does not come from the outside, but from an honest, whole-hearted acceptance and belief in who and what you are. But this was the first night of college and I yearned for the approval of my peers. In the room that night were many of the people whom I would come to know and love as the years went on.

I had little problem feeling comfortable around the girls. I still wanted their acceptance and friendship, but I realized early on that the true measure of my success was not going to be how many new girlfriends I made. It would be about my relationships with guys. My need for acceptance would crystallize into a need to be desired. There were a few guys in particular who stood out. Pat and Ed lived upstairs and were, to me, the definition of *cool*. They listened to Steely Dan and everyone seemed to gravitate towards them. But how many college boys (men, as I projected into a potentially lonely future) would find me desirable? I was like a teen mother, laden with responsibilities and a hard reality at an early age. I was always within sight of my chair, which, like children, was defining and fixed. It was a deal breaker.

Then there was Tom. Tom was from Pasadena and was one of those guys that just made you sigh when you saw him. He wasn't a male model by any means, but his white, toothy smile and straight dirty blonde hair caused all sorts of corny fantasies to run through my head. He looked like a good ole American boy, stood about 5'11" and was endowed with a lanky, muscular, swimmer's body. He was leaning against the frame of my door drinking a beer and every time he raised the bottle to his mouth the bottom of his T-shirt lifted just above the waist of his jeans, exposing his stomach and, from my vantage point, a little trail of dark blonde hair just below his navel. I guess he saw me looking in his direction, because he smiled and lifted up his bottle in the air as if to toast me. Needless to say, I made my way across the room, rolling over several feet in the process.

"Hi, I'm Carlana."

He flashed his beautiful smile and said, "I'm Tom. This your room?"

"Yup, sure is." I was so intrigued with him that I think I giggled.

"Lucky you: a single."

"Yea, I know. I guess I'm spoiled." I was hoping that he wouldn't connect the room to the chair, with some kind of need. My chair came with a world of needs: ramps, wide doorways, bigger spaces. I hated the idea of neediness. I wanted him to see me as someone in total control. The reality is that I did have special needs due to my condition. But I wanted the room to seem like a choice, a luxury. So I quickly did my best to take control of the situation.

"I begged my dad to get me a single this semester. Maybe next semester I'll get a share after I get to know some people. I didn't want to get stuck with some freak." I said it like I really had sat in front of my father pleading like a spoiled little girl for special treatment during my first year away at school.

"I totally know what ya mean. My parents would never foot the bill. It's great for parties," he said with a nod to the room.

"Definitely!" I said in an emphatic Valley Girl kind of way that was de rigueur back in the 80s.

Suddenly, I was shaken out of puppy love by what sounded at the moment like a butler of some kind demanding our attention. "Hello, I'm Tucker Hitchcock," Tucker said, as he sauntered over to us, emphasizing the H in Hitchcock ever so slightly.

"I'm Tom, nice to meet you." I don't think he quite knew what to do with Tucker. Most guys didn't. But Tucker looked rich and important and knew how to party, and at that stage in life, those attributes can carry you a long way. I could see him wondering if he heard his name right.

"Carlana, we've run out of tequila and I thought I'd just run down to the liquor store and buy another two-liter bottle and some ice," Tucker said with the kind of voice one might imagine a maitre d' using to discuss ordering a bottle of fine champagne.

Ever the charmer, he turned his attention to Tom. "Tom, are you drinking beer? Shall I pick you up a twelve-pack or perhaps a case?"

Tom declined his offer and studied him further. I am sure he had never encountered anyone like Tucker. Neither had I, for that matter. He was over the top. But I had been studying Tucker Hitchcock ever since he stepped into my room and though he seemed confident and vivacious, I sensed something dark about him that first day. Fear or sadness or perhaps both, I couldn't tell, but the feelings revealed themselves in fleeting facial expressions. In addition, his behavior pointed towards some kind of substance abuse. It was a great night and everyone was psyched about being away at school. We were all "on," so to speak. But he wasn't just on. His social stamina had an almost pathological quality to it. He was like a rabid social butterfly that flitted from person to person and group to group without coming up for air.

Poor Little Rich Kid: A Shared Woundedness

The night set the tone for my freshman and sophomore years. I established myself as a social butterfly, a girl that liked to have a good time. The following months would see one party after another, and my room became a fulcrum of social events. There was always someone or something hanging out, whether I was there or not. For a while it took on the feel of an opium den, as I'd often end up hosting cocktail parties that would run late into the night and end with people passed out on the floor. Tucker became a permanent fixture. He was always around for cocktails and always up. He had also become a close friend. He was there for me in ways that showed he understood me.

But I figured that I must have been successful in my desire to only show the parts of me that were the most attractive, since people seemed to be drawn to me. At least, that's what I attributed my popularity to. Within the first month or so, I became one of the best-known newcomers on the campus. I suppose any college freshman likes being around someone who's always ready to party, who's always on, and able to pay for Chinese food at one in the morning. It is interesting to think about the role of the chair in my persona. Looking back, no one so much as looked at it when they were speaking with me those first months. It was almost as if they were eager to play by my house rules and ignore it all together.

A few weeks into the semester, Gina, the girl whose long tan legs were always on display, knocked on my door. She just wanted "to chat," she said. We had become friendly and I invited her in to watch a show on my little fuzzy black and white TV. She seemed fine at first, but then turned to me as if she had something to say. Suddenly her composed exterior gave way to an expression of panic, revealing a psyche in distress.

"Oh my God, Carlana! I just can't believe it! He's such a shit!"

In my room, on my bed, the Rockette became hysterical. I did my best to console her. In between sobs I managed to find out that her boyfriend, the good-looking guy in the picture in her room, had cheated on her. She received a call from a friend back home informing her of the affair and had just confirmed it with him. He told her that he thought it would make sense "if they saw other people." She was devastated in the way that such statements have the power to devastate freshman girls. Or anyone else for that matter.

"Cheating on me! Can you believe it? I've turned down so many offers. I would never do that to him. I love him. We've been together for three years! I don't know what I'll do."

I held her tight and let her pour her heart out. For her I was a rock that could handle anything and was always in control. I was the one who would tell her everything would be okay and who she could believe.

"Listen," I said. "You are still you no matter what happens with him. You're still Gina, still beautiful."

"You think?" she pleaded, mascara running down her face, wanting me to tell her with absolute certainty that she would survive what, to her at least, felt like an insurmountable ordeal.

"Trust me," I said. "I know."

It was so ironic. Here I was, just weeks after arriving, worrying that people would find me as damaged goods, and the prettiest girl in the dorm was coming to me for support and understanding. It was probably my first inkling that my experience could offer something useful not only to me, but to others as well.

After Gina, there would be many others who would come to me under duress, like I was the resident psychologist. It was just how my condition played itself out. People felt like they could bare their souls to me. Everyone, ironically, except the one dearest to me. And to my eyes the one who needed to reach out most of all: Tucker.

As the semester wore on, he began to do a lot of drugs. Mostly cocaine, but other things too. In Boulder, recreational drug use was not uncommon. However, for Tucker at least, I know now that his drug use was a desperate act to mask his pain and gain acceptance. He kept all of his troubles bottled up inside and turned to drugs to keep his feelings from emerging. He was quite literally, and figuratively, numbing himself.

Despite his drug use, Tucker was there for me in ways that revealed a sensitivity to my inner struggle. He and I and our group of friends would often go out to one of the many clubs that offered live music. Nearly twenty years on, the nights are one big blur of drinking and rock and roll. I can recall sitting at the table and watching all our friends rush off to the dance floor in a mass exodus whenever the band played a popular song. I never expected anyone to stay behind to keep me company. But Tucker would always stay. And that's the bottom line. Whenever I found myself alone or feeling left out, I would turn around to find Tucker close by. At eighteen we were both old souls, a team. He made sure that I was never alone looking in.

Still, sometimes he drove me crazy. He was always trying to escape from reality through drugs or employ a strategic vagueness when he introduced himself to people so that they would think he was a Hitchcock of Hollywood lore when in fact he wasn't. He came from a society family in Palm Beach but it wasn't enough. He was so desperate for acceptance and affection that he fabricated a noble Anglo-American lineage in an effort to draw people closer to him. We were so similar. Tucker used fabrications and distortions to cope because he didn't feel comfortable with himself, and I hid my feelings from the world, never allowing myself or others around me an opportunity to mourn. We shared a woundedness and that's why we connected.

Life seemed full of joy and loving people, just as it always had been. People were still drawn to me in the way they were before the accident. There were sexy prom queens running to my room in tears, jazz tripping guys from Connecticut hanging around until all hours, and a Palm Beach dandy by my side at all times. But something was missing. It seemed that guys loved to be my friend, but couldn't bring themselves to see me in a romantic way. The chair kept love away from me. It seemed to me that men just couldn't handle it. I had met a few charmers in Boulder—Tom was one—whom I liked and felt might have held more than platonic feelings towards me, but no one had come to the fore. I was still as popular as ever though I had become a woman devoid of sexuality.

As time doggedly marched on and more of my friends entered into serious relationships, I began to feel like a spectator. I desperately wanted to feel attractive again, but sometimes, as the Rolling Stones say, "you can't always get what you want, but if you try sometimes, you just might find, you get what you need."

To Feel Desired

Winter break came and I went back home to Shreveport to spend the holidays with my family. It was great to go home, but I had made so many wonderful new friends that I hated the idea of leaving them. As much as they relied on me for a shoulder to cry on, or for a pep talk when they were feeling down, I relied on them to give me a sense of belonging and normalcy.

I had left home with a bit of trepidation about living so far away from friends and family. After the accident, their presence had meant so much to me. So I returned to Shreveport like a conqueror and was excited to tell everyone about my crazy parties and the new friends I'd made.

About five days after Christmas, I was in town shopping with my sister Mitzi. We split up and I ducked into a little shop to check out something that I saw in one of the big display windows. I was inside browsing when I heard a tapping sound. Someone was knocking on the window from the outside. I looked up expecting to see Mitzi, but instead found myself face to face with James.

I was stunned. I hadn't seen him in over six months. We had never really resolved things. After the accident we just kind of fizzled. No tears, no fighting, just icy cold avoidance. I don't think I ever got over the rejection I felt. He basically dumped me. I suppose he just couldn't handle seeing me and I am sure that there must have been a great deal of guilt on his part. I don't know, we never talked about it. He had visited me in rehab a few times, but my chair stepped in between us and when it was clear that it wasn't going to go away, he finally stopped calling.

He smiled and came into the store where we just stared at each other for a few moments, processing the past and the present. The accident and the shattering moment in the hospital when I first learned my life had changed came flooding back to me. I was inundated with a string of flashbacks that ran through my head like a movie stuck on fast forward: *I can't moo-ve! I can't breathe! You may never walk again.*

"I heard you were home," he said. He walked over, leaned down, and gave me a huge hug and kiss on the cheek.

"Hi, I meant to call you," I lied. I had no intention of calling him. His abandonment was still a raw subject for me. But looking up at him, I remembered the good times too. I remembered laughter and great kisses, something that I now worried I might never know again.

"You look really good," he said with a smile that was once reserved just for me.

We talked for a while about school and our families. We talked about mutual friends. Before we knew it, over an hour had passed and I was surprised to find that it was actually really nice to be with him again. Mitzi eventually found us and we said our goodbyes.

"What are you doin' tomorrow night?" he asked as we were leaving. "Let's grab some dinner."

I was thrilled. Gaining his acceptance was still of paramount importance to me. The next day came and he did call and we made plans to go out. I fussed and primped and tried to look my best. Later that night, he came to the door and chatted with my parents as I finished getting ready. His family had been so helpful after the accident, lending my parents their private jet to fly to Dallas and be with me in the hospital. I couldn't help but wonder if my father cringed a bit as we left the house. The last time James had taken his baby girl out, she came home in a wheelchair.

I felt a little awkward with my chair and took it apart in a matter of seconds in an effort to minimize the time he had to spend focusing on it rather than me. He put the chair in the trunk of the car and we were off to a nice Italian restaurant in town.

"You look great," he said again, with a smile on his face. He seemed to really mean it, even a bit surprised that he would find me attractive. I felt satisfied, since it was him, my high school sweetheart and boy who left me behind.

"Thanks," I said, lighting a cigarette and letting my arm hang out the window to catch the breeze.

That night at dinner he talked all about school in Austin and all the great people he had met. He started to talk to me about all of the college parties he had gone to. I just sat there waiting my turn. I eyed him closely. Here was the boy who was sitting next to me in the car the night my life changed. He was the one who organized the outing. He was fine. There wasn't a scratch on him and if you were to meet him you would never know that he was ever involved in any kind of accident at all. And there I was in my wheelchair, tethered forever to that night out and my ill-fated decision to get into that car. Once again, my mind drifted to the chaos just after the accident: James shouting, "Don't move!" frantic with concern. The burning pain in my legs. Then I settled back into the moment and rejoined time.

"So what's Boulder like?" he asked as he took a large sip of wine and steadied his eyes on me.

"Well, first of all it's beautiful. It's just below the mountains. And I've met so many great people there..." I proceeded to tell him all about Tucker, Gina, Pat, Ed, and of course Tom, whom I spent a little more time on than I really needed to just to see his reaction. I told him about my room being party central and all of the crazy nights that I'd hosted. He took it all in and I could see a sparkle in his eye. I knew that he was seeing me as the old Carlana that he thought he'd lost on the highway that night: full of life, the center of the party, everybody's best friend. As it often did, my bubbly, devil-may-care attitude was eclipsing my handicap. And restaurants were great camouflage for me as they were one of the few forums where everyone was sitting just like me and I could talk to people eye-to-eye. Sitting there across from him, I was just a pretty girl enjoying dinner with her date. The night felt like a relaxed stroll down a familiar road.

"It's really nice to see you again Carlana," he said to me as he pulled into my driveway.

"Yeah, it was nice," I replied with a true sense of satisfaction. It was the first time a boy showed a glimmer of interest in me since the accident. Granted, it was someone from my past, but he was still a boy and the way he looked at me in the car in front of my parents' house that night made me feel whole. It made me feel like a woman again.

There was a slightly tense silence and then he leaned over and kissed me. He kissed me softly and then he kissed me more, the way he used to kiss me when we would steal time away together and lose ourselves in each other's arms. I melted into him like a familiar dream and smelled his neck and touched is face.

He got the chair out of the trunk and we said our goodbyes. The next night was New Year's Eve and I would be going back to Boulder soon after.

"I'll call you tomorrow," he said.

When I rolled into the house that night I felt free. I felt like I had finally proved to myself that I could beat the chair on every angle. But victory and freedom, I would learn, are sometimes gained through acceptance and surrender.

The next night, on New Year's Eve, I celebrated like I had just won the lottery. My parents had a huge party for friends and family and I was on fire. My sister Mitzi kept asking why I seemed so pleased and I just smiled like the Cheshire Cat. At around 12:10, amidst all the hugging and kissing, the phone rang and it was for me. It was James. He was tipsy, as was I, but he was ecstatic.

"Hi you! Happy New Year!" he roared into the phone.

"Right back at ya," I chimed. My sister Mitzi just smirked at me. I took the phone into another room.

"Listen," he said. "Maybe we can see each other at school?"

"That would be so awesome!"

"I've never been to Boulder," he added, dropping a hint. It was crazy. One night with this boy and he had me again. I had forgiven him so easily for dropping me, for not being there when I really needed him most. I should have been hesitant and non-committal, but I plowed ahead just like I always did. I didn't care. I just wanted to be with him and to know that feeling again. To feel desired. "Why don't you come out for a long weekend?" I suggested.

He loved the idea. And over the next few days we agreed that he would fly out to Colorado in a couple of weeks.

Underestimating the Potential of the Heart

I returned to Boulder beaming with a newfound confidence and started planning my weekend with James. I told everyone about him and how we had reconnected. I told Tucker and all the girls on floor about the kiss in the car and how it felt almost as if we had never broken up. I had even taken a picture of him from home to show everyone what he looked like. I had it in a simple wood frame and placed it, shamelessly, on the bureau in plain sight of anyone who walked into the room. Now I was whole.

This was the proof, the badge that I needed to show everyone, to show myself, that I could be loved.

Tom stopped by on his first day back to say hello, knocking on my half-opened door and pushing it open before I could answer.

"Wow, he's a real looker," he said, motioning to the picture of James, his dirty blonde locks falling in front of his eyes.

"Hey, how are you!" I said, twisting my head and pursing my lips in a perfectly honed "you got me you little devil" stare.

"Guess I blew it," he said.

"That's James. He's my ex, sort of."

"Oh? I thought I was your only *sort of*?"

"You are...*sort of*," I said with a smile on my face.

"Bitch," he replied, bending down to give me hug and kiss and tell me about his break.

When you are feeling good about yourself, if something positive comes your way and the divine powers of the universe seem to scream "Yes!" in unison to your deepest hopes and desires, everything around you basks in the warm glow of affirmation. People look happier and healthier, trees and clouds seem like perfect creations and the sun shines just a bit brighter. Such was the case when I returned to Boulder in January. The entire town was bathed in a splendid light and it seemed more beautiful than ever before, because now I had become a more deserving and worthy participant in my surroundings.

The one blemish in my world was Tucker. Upon my return to Boulder, I saw a marked change in my chief pal and confidant. He looked dazed and his face was red and puffy with the strain of too much partying. He seemed listless and less engaged than before and every night he found an excuse to spend the night with me in my room. I didn't mind sharing my bed with him, but his behavior and appearance worried me. His pallor reeked of cocaine use. I asked if there was anything wrong and he shrugged and told me that he was fine. I felt like my mom dropping me off six months before and, like her, I studied him for a moment and let him have his space, understanding all too well what it felt like when you weren't ready to share the truth. I had grown very fond of Tucker though, and hoped that whatever was plaguing him, cocaine or some other burden, would soon lift.

Over the next week James and I finalized our plans. We spoke every night. It really was like someone had pressed rewind on my life and we were an item again. Every time we spoke, he had just come home from watching a football game or a frat party and had a mischievous, sexy manner of speaking egged on by a high blood alcohol level. He was a classic drunk dialer (though I too was guilty of a few such offenses). I would sometimes get calls late at night after he'd returned home from a bar because he "just had to call." He was sweet and made all kinds of references to how great it was going to be to spend time with each other. He was saying all the right things. Some of these calls even happened in front of other people, which I loved. We planned a party for the night of his arrival so that I could show him off and rejoin ranks of the loveable.

Before I knew it, two weeks had passed. Tucker had improved from those first few days and was back to his usual colorful self. When not lounging around my room watching what we could through the snowy reception on my small TV, he was running around like crazy inviting everyone to the party, which, of course, would be held in my room. Tom, Pat, Ed, and all the other guys were coming as were the girls on the hall. Even people from other dorms would be there. The party was shaping up to be a pan-university extravaganza. Pat and Ed, ever the event planners, had a stroke of genius one day and proclaimed, "We'll get a keg!" Tucker had some other tricks up sleeve.

James was arriving on Friday night, and on Thursday night I got another one of his late-night, drunken phone calls telling me how excited he was to come to Boulder.

"It's gonna be so sweet! I can't wait to get over there. God, I miss you."

"Me too! We've got a big party planned for Friday, so get ready," I said.

"Tomorrow night, seven o'clock, got my ticket right here. Don't be late."

"I won't be if you won't be," I told him. I was half expecting him to say, "I love you." He was so passionate and warm.

We had arranged to sneak the keg into Libby Hall and keep it in my room. By now, everyone in the dorm was talking about "Carlana's bash." The girls knew how much it meant to me. All week long they had held an informal countdown to James's arrival. Stephanie or Jen would stop by and look at his picture and say, "Two days..." and raise their eyebrows.

I'm not the neatest person around and with Tucker staying with me so often and being party central, my room was a total disaster. I had planned a marathon cleaning session before his arrival on Friday, but I came back from class that afternoon to find my room spotlessly clean. There were even cut flowers on a perfectly made bed. On my pillow was a note from two amazing girls, BG and Missy, that said, "We love you Carlana!" I felt like the gods were trying to make up for all the pain and suffering that I'd gone through.

Out of all the girls, Gina was especially excited for me. She acted almost as if her ex-boyfriend was coming to visit. In honor of the event, she gave me a makeover. She even plucked my eyebrows, which helped give me a little lift.

"You are going to blow him away when he sees you tonight," she said, surveying her work.

I loved it. I felt like a girl again. I felt like I was on top of the world.

Gina left me at about three p.m. I did, indeed, want him to be blown away when he walked off the plane. She did a fabulous job, polishing me with all her LA beauty tricks. I was careful to choose an outfit that highlighted my best features, which meant a low-cut blouse. I chose a brown leather aviator jacket, a white blouse, a pair of new black Levis jeans that blended into the black seat of my wheelchair, and black cowboy boots. I was the master puppeteer, exposed on top and camouflaged down below.

I put on my favorite perfume, which at the time was Calvin Klein's Infinity, lit a cigarette, and just sat there. It was four p.m. I waited a half hour and at about 4:30 Tucker came bounding in carrying plastic cups and all manner of paraphernalia for the party.

"Carlana, this is going to be a great. James's going to be so impressed. Everybody's coming," he said as he put down the items on my dresser and lit a cigarette in one deft motion. He turned to look at me and smiled, "Wow, you look great. You're totally gonna get lucky tonight."

I snickered and raised my eyebrows. I was a good girl, but I was no Jessica Simpson. And while abstinence may be common these days, back in the eighties, sex, drugs, and rock 'n' roll were the norm. In my mind, I had built up the weekend to be an almost pivotal event in my life. *And why shouldn't it be with James, after all we'd been through*, I reasoned. That the weekend might be "the one" for me added to the nervous excitement of the occasion.

By five p.m. I was practically shaking with anticipation. The airport in Denver was about forty-five minutes away. I had planned to leave at 5:30 to ensure that I would be at the gate in time. I wanted to be right there when he got off the plane. The phone rang and it was Janet down the hall asking what time the festivities were due to commence. I could hear her munching on M&M's, her drug of choice. I told her to be in my room by seven thirty. I wanted everyone there when I brought James in. The phone rang again. This time it was Missy wondering if we needed anything. I told her no. Everyone seemed as eager for this night to get started as I was.

The phone kept ringing and all the calls started to make me nervous. There was too much activity and too many people asking me questions. I decided that it would be best to leave for the airport and sit in one of the bars. It would be kind of romantic to watch his plane pull in. Tucker would stay behind and set up the keg and other beverages. "I'll be back at about eight so make sure you're around to keep an eye on things," I told him. It was a bit like asking the fox to guard the henhouse.

I got my keys and made my way out of the room. Gina was walking down the hall. Her eyes opened wide when she saw me. "Are you on your way to the airport?"

"Yeah," I said.

"You look totally awesome!" she told me, giving me a thumbs-up like I was an airplane cleared for takeoff.

"Carlana, phone call!" I heard Tucker shout.

"Tell them I'll call them later," I shouted back without even fully turning around. "Bye!"

I wheeled away from Gina and continued to make my way down the hall.

"Wait a minute!"

"What?" I said, coming to a complete stop and tilting my head backwards with my eyes closed, waiting to hear what he wanted.

"It's James," he said.

I stopped and turned. Gina looked at me. It was 5:30 p.m. and he should have been in the air by now. I rolled back down the hall, retracing my route, and pulled into my room. Gina followed but didn't enter, standing at the doorway, blocked by intuition that the situation at hand was about to get ugly. Tucker was standing there with the phone in his hand. He looked concerned as he handed it to me. My heart was pounding in my chest.

"Hello?" I said.

"Hi."

"What's up? Aren't you supposed to be flying?"

"Yeah. Carlana, I wanted to call you earlier but I had some trouble with stuff here in Austin," he said. This time he was stone-cold sober.

"What kind'a trouble?" I asked, looking beyond Tucker to the dark January sky, the silhouette of the mountains barely visible in the dusk.

"Well, a friend of mine just broke his leg."

"Oh, that sucks. But why aren't you on your way?"

"Well, I just don't feel I should leave him right now...you know."

The strangest feeling was working its way from the pit of my stomach up through my body, rattling the metal rods in my back and vibrating into the tips of my fingers.

"Well, isn't there someone else who can stay with him?"

"No...well, yeah, but, you know he's kind of a good friend."

You miserable bastard! I thought. *You don't want to leave him because he broke his leg? I broke my back! What about me? I was alone!* I raged at him inside. But on the outside, Carlana, the stoic warrior, was holding up just fine.

"Oh, well, what about flying in tomorrow?" I said. I still wanted him to come. How could I tell everyone that he wasn't coming?

"Well, yeah, you know, I don't think I can."

"Why not? Really, there's plenty of stuff going on this weekend."

"Carlana," he said, interrupting me. There was a seriousness to his voice that I had never heard. "It's just not a good idea."

And with that I understood everything.

"Okay. I've got to go, James. I have a party to get ready for," I said, the tears welling up in my eyes. Tucker had already moved to close the door. Gina stood outside. I could see his reflection in the dark window as he shook his head from side to side like a doctor delivering bad news.

"I'll call soon," he said.

"Sure," I told him and I slammed the phone onto the receiver. My room, all decked out for a party to celebrate my return to womanhood, was silent and empty. It suddenly seemed like the unfortunate campaign headquarters of an unseated political candidate. Anticipated victory replaced by sorrow. The clang from the earpiece hitting the receiver echoed for a few moments, like my fading spirit.

In my despair, when I was once again feeling left behind from what was supposed to be a moment of joy, I turned to see my faithful ally sitting straight-faced on the side of my bed. Tucker was there.

"He can't make it," Tucker said, stating an obvious fact more than asking a question.

"No, he can't."

"Let's have a drink," he said immediately. He poured two rum and cokes and sat on the bed across from me.

"What did he say?"

"He said he couldn't come because one of his friends broke his leg." I said it looking down into the red plastic cup in my hands, the ceiling dimly reflected in the dark surface of my drink. Little by little, the cup and my hands were beginning to go out of focus. There was a burning sensation in my throat and I kept my head turned. The torrent was pushing against the dam and I couldn't hold it back any longer. The fear and frustration, the sense of loss, the anger, my father's mournful face, all these things came flooding over me like storm surge. The world was becoming blurry and there was nothing I could do to stop it.

"Oh," Tucker said.

"He told me a friend broke his leg," I said, looking up at Tucker. "Can you believe him? This is the guy who was with me in the car, Tucker. He was the one who put that night together. He left me sitting in a fucking hospital! He didn't come to me! And he has the nerve to make up an excuse about a guy who broke his leg!"

"Well, maybe it's really bad."

"It's not that, Tucker. He said he didn't think it would be a good idea. Do you know what that means? It means, when it came right down to it, he didn't think being with a girl in a wheelchair would be a good idea! He just couldn't bring himself to touch me! That's what it means!" I said, burying my face in my hands.

"Oh god, Tucker, I feel so stupid, going around here telling everyone about my great ex-boyfriend...showing everyone his stupid picture." I felt pitiful and pathetic.

When I looked up Tucker was looking right at me, his jawline set, listening intently. He came over from the bed and took my hands in his. Then he leaned in and hugged me. He held me tight and let me drain my pent-up sorrows all over his red cashmere sweater. I wept as quietly as I could, trying not to make too much noise. He didn't let go and stayed bent over so that he could put his arms around me. I felt so grateful for him.

"What am I going to do?" I asked him between sobs. "No one is ever going to love me. It's so unfair. I'm so tired of this damn chair. What did I ever do to deserve this chair?"

Tucker sat back on the bed and looked at me with as serious a face as I've ever seen. Then he said in a voice that lacked his usual airs, "You are my best friend. I love you more than you can possibly know."

"I love you too," I said. "You know that. But this is different. I feel damaged. Everyone is walking around so perfect. Everyone is falling in love. I feel unwanted and it hurts so much."

"Carlana," he said, "you have saved me. Do you understand? I know what it's like when it hurts so much you can't let it out." He took a sip of his drink and then looked at me, his eyes swimming in tears. "I..." he looked away.

"I've been hurt too," he said, bringing his hand to his forehead and hiding his eyes from view.

I suppose it was the moment. It was an opportunity to help and be helped. Because he then added, "I know what it's like to feel damaged. God, it's so hard, Carlana. I couldn't even begin..." he said, his voice trailing off. I felt the focus shift from me and knew that Tucker was about to reveal something he had never told anyone.

"Carlana, I was abused growing up."

"Oh Tucker, I'm so sorry. What happened. Did they hit you?" Suddenly my bruised ego didn't seem to sting so much. And in the middle of my anguish I made some room in my heart for Tucker. He shook his head no. Then he steadied himself and looked into my eyes, "They touched me."

He couldn't actually say the words, but I understood from the way he used the word "touch" that he wasn't referring to hugs and kisses. Having come from such a stable home, the idea of abuse, much less sexual abuse, never crossed my mind. I ached for him and reached out and hugged him.

"I want you to know this," he said, "to know that you're not alone."

He told me how a member of his family molested him repeatedly as a child. He had carried the pain around like a tumor since he was a boy. But it was finally out. I was the first person he had ever told. That night, our friendship transcended quiet understanding and reached a place of frank intimacy. Tucker and I had established a bond in the recent months and my rejection by James rang true with Tucker. In an effort to comfort me, he chose to reveal the horrible shame he felt about his abuse, the source of his own anguish. Together we found comfort that we were not alone.

We had finally shared the hard, raw details that were at the root of each of our pain. I was so happy he was there. He was my anchor that kept me from drifting into despair. What had started as a devastating moment had brought us closer together. It wasn't long before there was a knock on the door. The party would still go on. We would still go on.

"Hey, Carlana, you in there? We got a bunch'a booze out here." It was Pat. I told him to come back in fifteen minutes. Tucker and I looked at each other and gave each other one last hug.

"Thank you," I said.

"No, thank you."

"What am I gonna tell these people?"

Tucker was at his best when opportunities for cattiness presented themselves. "Oh that's easy," he said, lighting another cigarette. "Tell them he has a hernia and has to go in for emergency surgery. And every time you say it, mean it. Maybe it'll happen!"

"Hey, Carlana, we've got a keg out here and Gina doesn't want us to wait in her room anymore."

"All right!" I yelled back, dropping some Visine in my eyes. I opened the door and there were Pat and Ed, standing in their trench coats carrying the keg. Behind them Tom dragged a large plastic garbage can filled with two huge bags of ice.

"Jeez, Lana...where should we put it," Pat proclaimed in an exasperated voice as he and Ed lugged the sweaty silver keg into the room.

Before I could answer they set the keg up in an ice nest in the corner just by the door. Tucker stood by smoking nonchalantly, like a wealthy man watching the help. I think he might have held the door open with his index finger as they tromped by. It was now almost six and we still had a couple of hours before everyone was due to show up.

Ed and Pat took off but on his way out Tom did a double take and looked over.

"You're lookin' good," he said.

"Thanks."

"Aren't you supposed to be on your way to pickup dreamboat over here?" he asked, jutting his thumb out in the direction of James's picture like a hitchhiker thumbing for a ride.

"He's not coming." I said as matter of factly as possible.

"Oh, trouble in paradise?" he asked, with a serious undertone.

"Kind of," I glanced at Tucker, who was standing next him. He nodded his head as if to say, "go on, you know what to do."

"He has," I said, lowering my voice like I was about to convey a choice piece of gossip, "a hernia and has to go in for immediate surgery."

"Bummer," he said, wincing. "Guess I've got you all to myself. Catch you in a few."

"See ya."

"By the way, you look hot."

"Thanks," I said.

Eight o'clock rolled around and people started arriving in droves. There were at least twenty beer-swilling freshmen crammed into my room. By 8:30 another twenty were spilling out into the hallway. The guys, being young, self-involved, and intrigued by the keg, were largely indifferent to James's plight. Few asked where he was. But the girls wanted to know. "So, where is he?" they'd ask me. "Hernia," I would say, in a hushed voice. "Ew," was the usual response, noses crinkled as if a bad smell had just wafted into the room.

By eleven o'clock I had drowned my shame in an alcohol bath and was actually enjoying myself. Tucker never left my side. I noticed him offering cocaine to everyone and watched most people decline, some rolling their eyes when he turned his back to them. Weaknesses or not, he really was my best friend. I now had some insight as to why he resorted to self-destructive behavior. He was in desperate need of an escape.

At some point Ed yelled from across the room, "Hey, Lana, I heard your boyfriend's got damaged goods!"

"Yeah, I'm exchanging him for a new model," I barked back.

"Right on!" Gina screamed, high-fiving me. She knew full well that this guy had hurt me and was probably drawing parallels to her own love life. She then bent down to hug my neck and kiss my cheek.

"You are awesome," she whispered in my ear.

"Damaged goods," I thought. "They think that *he's* damaged goods."

The party wrapped up at around 2:30 a.m. and amazingly I didn't get scolded by the administrators. I couldn't have cared less anyway, as I felt I was due a little compensation for my disappointment. After everyone left, I jumped into my bed, pushing off some detritus from the festivities, and called it a night. Despite James not showing up, I managed to have a great time with the people around me. I appreciated Gina's show of solidarity because it meant that she felt a camaraderie with me, that we were in the same boat. I appreciated Ed's comment because it showed that he didn't think of *me* as damaged. Most of all, I thanked God for Tucker. It was becoming apparent to me that I might have underestimated the potential of the eighteen-year-old heart.

Lesson Learned: *A Shared Experience*

Sometimes life can make us feel like we are islands. When we experience a tragedy or loss, it can feel like we are the only ones who could possibly understand our pain and suffering. After I had my accident, I used to think that I was marked. That somehow the accident wasn't just an event with a beginning and an ending clocked in seconds on a highway. For me the accident was like a brand that was seared into me and forever set me aside from everyone else. I felt like the survivor of a disease that everyone stays away from long after the illness has wreaked its havoc.

I thought that for most people, my physical presence evoked pain and suffering, emotions that people didn't want to deal with. I didn't think that anyone would ever want to get close to me because it would mean dealing, even in the most abstract way, with loss.

Encountering new people in Boulder taught me that we all have our burdens to bear. At first everyone seemed unscathed. But over time, I began to realize that people kept their pain hidden inside placid exteriors. And that my popularity had as much to do with my adversity acting as a conduit for honest communication as it did my outgoing nature. I realized that, like our joys, suffering and grief were two human experiences that connected us all.

Gina, who came to me with her boyfriend troubles. Tucker, my dearest friend, who shared his pain and shame with me. They are just two of the many people who felt comfortable telling me their stories and the dark things that they kept hidden away from the world. I had unbelievable amounts of fun in Boulder, but it was a learned appreciation of the commonality of our experience that gave me hope.

I do not wish to generalize suffering in any way. There clearly are degrees of pain and loss. As I write this, the nightly news is filled with images of young men and women who have been killed in Iraq. I'm an aunt and know enough parents to understand that losing a child is like dying a little. Such a loss is staggering and final. But while our tragedies may not be the same, the emotions they generate are all shades of the same experience. If you are suffering right now, know that you are not alone. Try to reach out to people. Nobody is going to take your pain away, but there is solace in knowing that people understand. Grief, like joy, is a universal experience.

WE ARE NOT ALONE IN SUFFERING OR GRIEF

The bombing of the World Trade Center on 9/11 was a horrific event, which resulted in staggering loss. Aside from the loss of life, in an instant we as a nation lost our sense of security and our financial stability. All seemed shattered. The tragedy caused many of us to examine our lives and question the future.

When we lose a family member or friend or loved one, we lose not only a part of ourselves, but also our vision of the future. The family is forever different because of the loss and pain it suffers. During my work as a producer in Hollywood, I researched an organization born out of 9/11 and the amazing family behind it. I was so impressed by this family's reaction to an incomprehensible tragedy that I want to share their story.

On September 11, 2001, Ron Fazio Sr. witnessed a plane crash into the WTC1 building. From the ninety-ninth floor of the WTC2 building next door, he watched in horror as a second plane seemed headed directly for his office. He quickly warned everyone to get out as fast as they could. He held the door open to ensure his friends' and coworkers' safe exits and then searched the entire floor to make sure that everyone made it out. That was the last time Ron was seen alive.

Ron Fazio Jr. told me, "My dad was a quiet, humble man who died after holding the door open for others. As a family, we're trying to do the same thing and help people move through the pain so they can begin to dream again."

Ron Fazio Sr.'s family has put together a living memorial to him: Hold the Door for Others, Inc., a non-profit organization dedicated to helping others cope with the pain of loss and begin to heal and move on.

Ron Jr., thirty-one, is studying for his doctorate in psychology and heads up the project. They have assembled a team of psychologists and grievance and career counselors to help victims of tragedies move past grief and begin to live again.

Regardless of what kind of loss we're facing, there is that awkward period when we are left standing between a closed door and the one that has yet to open—standing between the past and what lies ahead. The transitional period between these two doors occurs when we experience our grief. It is a difficult and turbulent time but it marks a new beginning.

Sometimes we are so fixated with our loss that we fail to notice the open door before us. The Fazios are living proof that we can reach out to people during periods of grief to help find our way into the next phase of life. They understand that there is a commonality to our experiences and that we are not alone. And that when tragedy strikes, there is an insight that we must unearth from the experience.

If you are not ready to involve friends or family in your troubles, or can't for some reason, I guarantee that you could find a group or organization somewhere that offers access to people going through a similar experience. Find them. Don't hesitate. Trust me: it will shorten the time that you are in acute pain and take some of the fear away.

Create a virtual memorial

Losing a loved one is always difficult to endure. But there are some things we can do to celebrate the lives and personalities of those we've loved and lost. Find a permanent home for the memorial. Today you can find places on the internet where you can share the sentiment with other loved ones all over the world. You can find places that will print your text for free or for a minimal fee; you can arrange a memorial with sound and images combining to tell others about someone they never knew and how they touched those around them.

By celebrating the memories, you will feel empowered and find great joy in telling others about your loved one and why they were so special. It is a beautiful, timeless tribute. You will feel comforted and the pain will lessen. The memories will be your company. You will find yourself reflecting on the good times and all the happy memories you made with the person you've lost. And you will know that you are not alone.

· · · ·

Practice random acts of kindness

Make a daily list of things you could do to make someone else smile: buy a stranger a cup of coffee; visit a someone confined to a home or hospital; read a book to a child; phone a friend; skip a lunch and give your food to a homeless person. Make every day really count. It feels so good to help someone else, doesn't it? By doing little things like this we are also letting others know that they are not alone. What better feeling is there to share with someone?

When you shift your energies towards a noble mindset, your own troubles will seem to melt away. When we practice random acts of kindness, everyone benefits. You are always in a win-win situation.

CHAPTER 4

Learning to Have Faith in Others

· ·

Spying on the Living

Sometimes the road to recovery involves painful twists and turns. During the spring semester, I made another trip home to Shreveport to attend a wedding. The daughter of my mom's best friend was marrying one of Shreveport's most eligible sons. It was a huge social event and it was held at the country club. Everyone who was anyone in town was there. I attended with my parents, along with my two sisters, Mitzi and Karen. I wore a beautiful black dress, which besides being event-appropriate camouflaged my ever-thinning legs.

It seemed the entire town had come together to celebrate that night. The town and the club house seemed enchanted with the addition of fine gowns and matrimonial regalia. Everyone seemed enveloped by the pageantry of the event. I looked good and felt attractive.

Like a soldier on leave, I let myself sink into the warmth of the moment. I had been working so hard to maintain myself, to stay positive, and as a result my life had continued despite my chair and skinny legs. But unfortunately, as is often the case, soldiers cannot afford to let their guard down, not even for a moment.

As the evening reached its crescendo, the band played music perfect for slow dancing. The dance floor was packed. I had just snuck outside for a cigarette and was sitting near the entrance of the ballroom. Looking around the room, I saw my mom in a corner speaking to one of her friends. My two older sisters and my father were nowhere to be found. The lights were dim and flickering candles gave the room a dreamy quality.

Then I saw them. Out of the collage of people on the dance floor, I saw my father and my sister Mitzi slow dancing. They were enjoying a wonderful moment together as father and daughter. They danced gracefully across the floor, my father beaming with pride as he looked down at his daughter. The song segued into another sentimental melody and as it did I could see my father scanning the room, looking for something, and then I watched as a broad smile crept across his face. His eyes had come to rest upon my sister Karen. He held out his arm, gesturing her forward, and she walked out to meet him. Again, father and daughter shared a tender moment. I watched like a ghost spying on the living.

The song changed tempo and Karen kissed him on the cheek. He stood on the edge of the dance floor and scanned the crowd once more. He searched and searched until his eyes found me. Except this time, there was no smile. The scene seemed to unfold in slow motion.

I wanted to look away or hide, but I just sat there, frozen and terrified of the storm of feelings that was welling up inside of me.

The moment seemed to hang there forever and it was as if our hearts were connected and saying all the things we could not bear to speak. A stream of emotion flowed between us. The pain. The helplessness. The anger. *Oh Daddy, I'm so sorry!* I screamed inside.

All the frustrations, all the guilt for hurting the people I love, all the agony of losing a future, and all the fear of being cast aside, all of it came boiling up and there was no stopping it. I turned and rolled myself as fast as I could out of the room and down the hall towards the bathroom. I didn't want anyone to see me break down. I didn't want to cause any more suffering. I just wanted to grieve. As my wheelchair rushed forward, echoes of that fateful night crept into my mind and those horrible words, *"You may never walk again."* I felt I could take the pain when it was just me in the ring, but I couldn't live with the thought of my father or mother suffering because of me. No matter how stoic I was, there was nothing I could do to protect them. Tears streamed down my face. I felt responsible for everything.

When I reached the bathroom, I found a stall, locked the door, and silently sobbed. "What have I done! What have I done!" I repeated over and over. I heard the bathroom door open and my sister Mitzi calling my name. She had come for me.

"Carlana, are you okay? Let me in."

"I'm fine," I said. There was no way I was going to make her suffer any more than she already had. I had just begun to let out some of the pain. But once again, I summoned the soldier inside of me and pulled myself together. I shuddered, my body jerking forwards and backwards as if trying to hold in a deep cough. I picked my heart up off of the floor, wiped my eyes, and came out of the stall with as much pride as I could manage.

"You want to talk? Are you okay?" Mitzi pleaded.

"I'm fine. I just need a minute." I went over to the mirror and reapplied my makeup.

"I wish you would just let me help."

"I'm fine," I said with an emphatic tone conveying that the matter was closed. And with that I ushered her out of the bathroom and we rejoined the party.

The event was never discussed again.

I regained my composure that night and the next day I woke feeling a little shaken, but in control. When I went to breakfast that morning, no one looked at me strangely or gave the slightest hint that anything had happened the night before. Sometimes, it's just easier to avoid a subject when there really is nothing that can be done. No amount of talking or crying would make me walk again. For my family, pain was just something that we had learned to live with and it sat amongst us like an unwanted guest.

While the dam held, my breakdown at the wedding revealed just how much pain I was keeping at bay. I was tortured by guilt. By the suffering and grief that I had caused everyone. But in hindsight, there was more going on that night than knowing I might never dance with my father again. My inability to glide across the dance floor like my sisters only served to reinforce my growing apprehension about my prospects, or lack thereof, for finding love. My condition seemed to disallow so many of the symbolic rituals associated with courting and romantic rights of passage. It was painfully clear that I was on the outside of normal. It was as if I was the only one who still saw me as a sexual being. I suppose people thought the paralysis took away my desires. It didn't.

All of Me

I returned to Boulder feeling like I had taken a step backwards. The overwhelming feeling of inadequacy that had greeted me on my arrival months before had returned. I didn't think that there was anything that could counter the blow I received at the wedding.

Not long after my fateful trip home and still under its melancholic spell, my friend Joe invited a group of us for a ski weekend in the mountains. It was his parents' place near the resort town of Breckenridge. I had seen pictures and heard all about it but had never actually been up there. Joe and the others were all leaving on Friday evening. My friends Pat and Ed were going. Missy, Eric, and handsome Tom were planning to go too. Tucker and I planned to drive up together after class.

The Thursday night before the trip, Tom stopped by my room for a surprise visit. "Hey you, is there room for me tomorrow? I heard you drive like a bat outta hell," he said with a hearty smile on his face.

"Yeah, sure; it's just gonna be Tucker and me," I told him.

We chitchatted some more and he bid me farewell. But before he left, he stopped in my door and looked back at me. "You okay?" he asked questioningly.

"Yea, I'm fine," I said.

The next day Tom, Tucker, and I drove up to Joe's mountain house. Tucker, who had crawled back to my room at about 4:30 a.m., slumbered in the back seat. Tom rode shotgun and was completely mystified by the hand controls that I used to drive my car. The drive up to the ski resort from Boulder took us through spectacular, serpentine canyons that followed mountain streams.

The road was flanked by snow-capped peaks. It called for slow driving but I got into the curviness of the road. People are sometimes surprised to find that I am not a defensive driver. If you see a black convertible sports car screeching through a yellow light at the corner of Sunset Boulevard and Sweetzer Avenue in West Hollywood, it's probably me. I am polite about it though, and always thank the people I cut off.

With Tucker unconscious in the back seat, I talked to Tom the whole way to Breckenridge. I enjoyed the time I spent with him and we got to know each other better. Road-trips encourage intimacy. He really was a terrific guy. He had grown up comfortably in Pasadena but had worked all summer to help pay for his school (something he would do for his entire college experience). He was a gifted writer and aspired to be a journalist (he ended up becoming a real estate developer, but this was freshman year and anything seemed possible). I remember him saying, "I kind of think you need to fight for things to really appreciate them."

"I know what you mean," I told him. "Sometimes though, it's kind of nice to take a leave from the battle, but every time I do, I seem to take a hit."

He smiled, reached over, and squeezed my hand.

We arrived at Joe's mountain lodge at around two in the afternoon. Tucker rose, zombie-like, out of the back seat, the circles under his eyes made darker in the brightness of all the fresh snow. It was a true winter wonderland. There were giant pine trees and cute lodges all around. In front of the house, I could see an amazing vista of snow-capped mountains flanked by evergreen forests. Tom gave me a piggy back ride into the lodge and

Tucker carted in my chair. Inside, our friends had already set up for the long weekend. Joe, Ed, Pat, Missy, and Eric were all sitting around the fireplace drinking. Tom plopped me down on the couch and then brought us each a beer.

"Drives like Mario Andretti," he informed the group, looking at me with pride and clinking his bottle to mine.

"To Mario!" everyone cheered. Missy belched.

The house was fairly new, not rustic as I was expecting. It had natural wood siding and that off-white interior that was so popular in houses built in the eighties. But it was charming nonetheless. A high ceiling graced a large living room, which gave it a chalet-like feel. There were three bedrooms and a porch off the front of the house that overlooked the pristine landscape. I imagined it would be a nice place to sit and drink wine during the summer months. The house, being new, was filed with a pleasant scent of cut wood. The only feature that I didn't care for was its biggest attraction: a Jacuzzi tub on the second floor that could seat five people. Jacuzzis meant bathing suits, and bathing suits meant revealing my body.

Outside, the snow picked up and the day was already starting to turn to dusk. In the mountains you can be out of direct sunlight well before the sun dips below the horizon. We were all together around the warm fireplace, just hanging out.

I looked around at my circle of friends. I thought back to Shreveport, the wedding, and then looked at myself sitting with all these wonderful, warm people. All new additions to my life. I had worried so much about being pitied, about being compromised by my condition. But the feeling that wrapped around me like a comfortable old family quilt wasn't pity, it was acceptance and love. I suppose it was because I was outside of Boulder that it hit me: we, all of us, had chosen to be together. These people were not mere acquaintances, they were good friends. I enriched their lives as much as they did mine. We grounded each other.

In talking to Tucker, counseling Gina, and sharing with Tom, I was beginning to feel that it might be safe to let the world see me: all of me. The sting from James's rebuff was already subsiding. Deep in the Rocky Mountains on a snowy night during my freshman year in college, I felt whole. I didn't need any guy to accept me in order to validate my being.

Tucker finally came to and was his usual entertaining self. He was always the life of the party, narrating the evening with his unusual brand of catty commentary. No one was safe. It was kind of like having Truman Capote over for dinner.

With a snowstorm raging outside, the consensus was to cook lots of food, drink lots of wine, and play games. For college kids, we were well endowed with credit cards and a taste for good food, thanks to our parents' success and epicurean tutelage. We managed to procure top quality steaks and seafood. Eric and Missy brought up some superb California wine, which we drank far too fast. Dinner was served casually in front of the fire and we soon found ourselves savoring a well-earned food coma, our blood warmed and stomachs satiated. It wasn't long before someone broke the peace and uttered the inevitable: Jacuzzi. Missy cheered. I cringed.

Everyone disappeared into the bedrooms to chuck their clothes and put on boxer shorts or bathing suits. I didn't bring anything that was appropriate and, despite my earlier warm thoughts about my friends, was horrified at the idea of showing everyone my body. My legs were skinny and pale. To me, they looked skeletal. There was no way that I could get into the tub without help. That meant my legs would be dangling in front of everyone until they were finally submerged and hidden in the churning water. It meant that everyone was going to be given a full dose of what paralysis looks like up close. I tried my best to get into the mood and assure myself that the people who would be sharing the tub with me were confidantes. Unfortunately, it didn't do any good and I reluctantly took my pants off and put on one of Tucker's t-shirts, which hung on me like a muumuu and provided some covering over my thighs.

Tucker and I were going to sleep down by the fireplace, so after changing, there I sat in the sunken living room, looking up to a loft above us, and waiting to be hauled upstairs in my steel palanquin. Missy leaned over the railing of the loft and looked down into the living room. "You comin?" she asked, her long dark hair hanging down like a mane.

"Yeah, but I need a hand."

"What about Tucker?" she asked. Tucker was sitting next to me in a daze, having successfully numbed himself to his previous hangover by drinking a bottle of wine.

"Well, he needs a little help," I said.

"Yeah, I guess so...Tom!" she yelled, taking a swig off a freshly opened beer.

A second later Tom thumped down the stairs wearing nothing but his flannel boxers. He was beautiful. Nearly six feet tall, his body was smooth and slightly tan from winter break in Pasadena. He was the portrait of the California boy, with sandy brown hair and a lanky build. He looked at Tucker, raised an eyebrow, and looked at me. Then without saying anything he leaned over me, put one arm under my knees and the other under my arms.

"Oh!" I said, "don't hurt yourself!"

"You kidding me?" he responded, his face next to mine.

I instinctively wrapped my arms around his neck and in one fell swoop he lifted me out of my chair and proceeded to carry me up the stairs and into the bathroom, setting me down on the side of the Jacuzzi. The whole time he carried me, I had the pleasure of nuzzling against his neck. I could smell him; a combination of sweat and the slightest hint of smoke from stoking the fire earlier.

I lowered myself into the tub. No one was there. "Well, you are quite the athlete."

"Swimming, four years in high school." He flexed like a weightlifter, mocking himself.

"I see," I said. "Well come on in, water's great."

He took a seat next to me and Tucker quickly followed suit. Tucker was actually very well built, despite his laziness and constant partying, due to years of playing tennis. I just couldn't imagine the Tucker I knew running around on the tennis court. Time had not diminished the results of those years of working out. His calves were strong and well defined. He sank into the bath, totally unphased by Tom's slight downstairs and I put an arm around him. I held Tucker close, ever-aware that my best friend was suffering from a deep wound, inflicted long before the drugs ever arrived on the scene. And Tucker offered a sense of comfort at what was for me such an awkward moment. Missy came bounding in first, followed by the guys. The room had wood paneling and there was a window through which you could see a giant pine tree waving in the howling wind and blowing snow. It was quickly covered with condensation from the Jacuzzi. All the lights were turned off and several candles were lit. I remember it all so clearly, that night, that tub.

The conversation was animated. The guys were fixated on the skiing they would do the next day. Joe described in detail the various trails that snaked through the nearby ski areas. We had all gone there to ski, even me. I had a specially designed device called a mono-ski, which was in essence a seat mounted on a ski that I used to maneuver down the mountain. It came with short poles with small skis at the end which I used to help control myself. It was actually pretty high tech for the time and provided me the luxury of an activity which took me out of the wheelchair.

Everyone's attention was focused on Joe as he described a bowl high atop a nearby mountain. I had never skied above the tree-line and was really excited about being on a huge, white expanse with no boundaries. I imagined that it would make me feel free, like I was flying.

"Doesn't that sound awesome?" I said, turning away from Joe and looking at Tom. But Tom didn't respond. He was staring at me with a consuming look. The kind of look that someone has when they are savoring an object of desire. I could tell that he had been watching me for some time and when my eyes met his, it was like he was speaking to me. He had an almost surprised look on his face. *I had no idea,* he seemed to be saying. The world went silent and I looked down at the bubbling water, my face kissed by the steam, and then back up at Tom, smiling involuntarily.

All the guys were still yapping away about skiing and had segued into the best strategy for attacking moguls. They hadn't noticed our silence. Tucker was on the other side of me trying to feign interest in the mogul debate. But Missy was sitting on the edge of the tub with her feet in the hot water drinking her beer, looking down at me with just the slightest smirk on her face. She had tuned in. Tom's hand reached through the water to clasp mine.

Before long the beer, food, and warm water had taken their toll. "I'm outta here," Joe declared. With that, the guys got out almost simultaneously, continuing their ski technique debate until they left the bathroom and made their way to their respective rooms. Tucker got up too and when he did Missy grabbed him by the arm and took him into the other room. I heard her whispering and figured that she was greasing the wheels of romance.

Tom and I sat in the Jacuzzi alone.

"You want to get out?" he asked, caressing my arm just below the surface of water.

"In a minute. I kind of like it in here," I said.

"Me too," he said, rubbing his thumb against my arm with a back and forth motion.

My heart was pounding with the anticipation of imminent contact. My body and soul knew that they were about to be touched, embraced by another.

He looked up towards the door, which Missy almost closed on her way out. Then he looked back at me and leaned in close and kissed me. It was soft and gentle. I kissed him back and wrapped my arms around his neck for the second time that night. We sat there for nearly a half hour more, until the voices died off and the house went dark save for the glow of the fire still burning in the stove below. Until I was sitting in his lap, kissing him with my whole being.

"Let's go down by the fire," he whispered.

"I'm soaked. I need to get out of these things."

"Me too," he said with a grin.

I pulled myself up onto the side of the Jacuzzi and grabbed a nearby towel. Turning away from him, I peeled off my wet shirt and wrapped the towel around me just below my breasts so that I gained maximum coverage for my thighs. (I was not modest per se, I just wanted to cover up my skinny legs.) Tom jumped out of the warm water, shivered vocally, and wrapped himself up in a big towel, taking off his wet boxers underneath. He tied the towel around him like a sarong and then disappeared from the room. I heard him tromping down the stairs once more and a few minutes later he made his way back up to me.

"You ready?"

I honestly didn't know. Ready for what? I mean, here I was with this guy that, until one hour ago, I would never have imagined would want to be with me. We flirted, we hung out at parties, and we talked in a car, but so what? He was perfect; he could have had anyone. I had wanted so much to be seen as a young, sensual woman, that now that it was happening, I was a bit unprepared. So I responded accordingly. "Ready if you are," I said.

He leaned in and picked me up again. His skin was warm from the tub and slightly damp. He seemed to pull me in closer than before, the stubble from his day-old beard brushing against my cheek. Carefully he made his way with me down the stairs. I was worried that Tucker might interfere, but to my relief, he was nowhere to be found (I think even Tucker knew to give us our time). The fire in the wood-burning stove drenched the room in a soft yellow light (the lighting is always so perfect in this memory!). Where there was once a coffee table was now a down comforter, laid directly in front of the stove so that it sat in a valley created by the sofa and two love seats. Outside, the wind rattled the sliding glass doors that opened onto the porch in the front of the house.

He put me down on the comforter and lay down next to me, checking on the stove. There was a blanket on the loveseat, which I immediately pulled off and spread over me, hiding my legs from sight and using it as a blind behind which I could take off my wet bottoms. I lay back on one arm, still wrapped in my towel. I felt the warmth of the stove against my skin.

Tom leaned into me. He wrapped his strong arms around me and pulled me to him. There was no pity in his action, just desire. The towel fell from my body and I felt his skin against mine. His hands squeezed me hard and then caressed me softly. Looking at me, now supine, he took his hand and tried to lift the blanket from my lower half.

"Wait," I said.

"Are you okay?" he whispered.

"I'm more than okay," I said, kissing his slightly parted lips.

"What's the matter then? I want to see you. All of you," he said.

"Nothing's the matter," I replied, looking away.

"Then why are you clutching the blanket?"

I suppose it was the honesty of the moment. Or maybe something had changed in me that night, because without hesitation I blurted out my fear.

"But my legs, they're so not sexy."

"What?" he said, looking at me, confounded.

"I mean, they're so thin. I'm just a little self-conscious."

"Carlana, you're beautiful," he said softly, his towel slipping slightly as he reached to lift my blanket and join me.

"Wait," I said, grabbing his hand. All of a sudden the world was rushing in at all sides. It was as if I had been standing on a rock in the middle of a river and the water was rising all around me, consuming my patch of safe ground. I panicked and he'd seen it.

"What's the matter?"

"I can't. I'm sorry, Tom. I can't." I just couldn't do it. Despite the confidence that I had been feeling, I just wasn't ready to share myself in that way. I was too self-conscious about my body to allow Tom or anyone else that level of intimacy. I wasn't ready to leave my safety zone.

"Why?"

"I just can't," I said, looking at him with pleading eyes.

He looked at me for what felt like several minutes. "It's okay," he said finally, as if concluding the issue, my issue. He drew close to me, wrapping his arms around me. "I'm sorry," he added.

"Don't be," I said. "It's not you. I'm the one who's sorry."

After a while he said, "You know, I don't even think of you as being handicapped."

I laughed uncomfortably. "Thanks Tom," I said irreverently. It was clear that I did!

"What I mean is, I don't see you that way."

"Thanks. I wish I could say the same," I said softly.

We lay together by the fire all night long. While I didn't give myself to him physically, I did share myself with him. I told him what really happened with James at Christmas and how it made me feel. He in return listened and offered me a story about being humbled by a girl from home. But it was a moment of reckoning for me. I was flattered and reassured by Tom's affection. But I was also frustrated with my own insecurity and realized that in hiding my pain from the world I was really hiding it from myself. It may just have been possible that I was the one who couldn't be trusted with the truth, with the reality of my situation.

Back in the USSR

Before I knew it, nearly a year had passed since our weekend in the mountains at Joe's lodge. My friendship had deepened with Tom and everyone that was there. In fact, as the semesters wore on, my life seemed dominated by socializing rather than schoolwork.

After that evening with Tom, I entered into a self-imposed state of celibacy. I just couldn't share myself on that level. It didn't matter because no other guy had expressed a serious interest in me anyway. I expected to spend my entire college career in Boulder well endowed with friends yet very much alone in terms of romance.

On a Sunday afternoon during sophomore year, I received a phone call that would once again change my life.

"Hey precious!"

"Hi, Dad!"

My father is a brawny southern gentleman with a huge heart and a commanding, instantly recognizable voice. We bantered back and forth a bit, but his manner became serious and I quickly realized that this was no father-daughter courtesy call.

"Darlin', you ever heard of stem cells?" he asked me.

"No."

"It comes from a fetus."

"Gross."

"Yeah, but these cells, I've been talking to some doctors that think they might be able to help you."

"What do you mean *help me*?"

He paused. "I mean, cure you."

My mouth went dry. The idea of a cure had always remained in the back of my head. But I had lived such a great, full life in Boulder that I put my physical future on the back burner. He spent the next fifteen minutes explaining the concept of using fetal cells to bridge a break in a spinal cord. It was fascinating and the science sounded good. The concept made sense.

"How do I do this? Where do I go? Where are the doctors?" I asked eagerly.

"Well, that's the complicated part honey. They're in the Soviet Union."

Lesson Learned: *Trusting Others*

Sometimes when life throws a curve ball at us, especially when that curve ball leaves a physical mark, we turn inward. It's almost as if we feel that our acknowledgment of our own frailty, our wounds, will make them worse or point to a weakness inside of us that will render us undesirable. We become islands at the times when we should be building bridges and reaching out for help.

When I think back to the period just after the accident, at my behavior, I see a frightened young woman trying to survive. I tried to hide my pain from the world because I worried the world would toss me out like damaged goods if it knew how bad it really was. I did not trust in the capacity of others to see with their hearts. It is ironic, because what I wanted more than anything was for them to trust in me. To trust that I was whole and good and not an invalid. To trust that I was still beautiful.

My experience in the mountains with Tom and my friends led to an epiphany. I realized after months of fearing rejection, that people, even young, self-possessed eighteen-year-olds, were able to see beyond my chair. They found me as someone with whom they could relate, and with whom they could reveal themselves. Not as someone defined by limitations, but a person with the potential to enrich their lives and be a good friend. They found me whole. My fears of rejection were really reflections of my own prejudices.

As a result, I felt better about who I was and more comfortable sharing myself with the world, both my weak and strong points. I realized that I could lean on people because they loved me and wanted nothing but the best for me. They didn't pity, they simply wanted to be included. As the days and weeks passed, I developed strong bonds with Tom and many other friends.

Avoidance, concealment, distraction, call it what you will. Hiding your true self from the world around you, especially when you are facing adversity or going through hard times, keeps you from the valuable resources that are your friends and family. People that can help you move forward and get to the place that you are going with a little less stress and anxiety. My European friends like to tell me, "In America you have psychiatrists, in Europe we have neighbors." That's a dose of Old World sensibility that I think we should all take to heart.

BELIEVE IN THE ABILITY OF OTHERS TO SEE WITH THEIR HEARTS

My adversity centered on my physicality. However, there are many events in life that can make you turn inward. Recovering from a breakup or an abusive relationship can cause us to feel ashamed and undesirable. It's important to realize that these feelings and the resultant distorted reality that nurtures them are self-perpetuated. Picking up the phone and reaching out to a friend or family member to help you carry your burden is the one of the smartest things you can do. They will help you gain perspective and find the road back. They will help make sure that your shame or grief does not become destructive, as in the case of Tucker's cocaine use. In your mind, think of three people. One of them can serve as your lifeline. Don't hide your pain from the world.

Living Proof: *Coming Out*

For many people coming out is as frightening as it is liberating. My dear friend David came out to me when we were in college. I was touched that he trusted me with such a personal secret.

David told me that he felt like a prisoner. He had tried to be what everyone wanted him to be—heterosexual. Many of his friends were women, but he always found himself sexually as well as emotionally attracted to other men. Hiding the fact that he was gay became more and more emotionally draining. He hated pretending to be straight, talking about girls and making up sexual experiences just to fit in. The idea that he would have to behave that way for the rest of his life was deadening. Sometimes he admitted that the pain of living a lie was so great the he would cry himself to sleep at night.

Hiding a major aspect of your identity is humiliating and fosters self-loathing. As long as you're not hurting other people, you've done nothing wrong. It seems to me the only truly "wrong" course of action is to hide who you are.

He wanted to feel free. Coming out was a very liberating experience for him. Even after coming out to himself and the important people in his life, he has found the process to be a lifelong journey. Gay people must make coming-out decisions in the workplace, with health care providers, and even in places of worship. Coming out truly is a never-ending journey.

It never ceases to amaze me that we have such an ability to limit ourselves with our paralyzing fear. We tell ourselves over and over again that we are not normal, that we will not be accepted or tolerated. So often, we torture ourselves with a horrific vision of the future. Sometimes we can be our own worst enemies. This was the case with David. But he finally decided that he was the one in control of his life and that anyone who didn't accept him as he really was didn't really love him in the first place.

When his family and the rest of his friends learned David was gay, a most remarkable thing happened. They embraced him. Some needed a little time to adjust to the new reality that he was presenting. But they became more open and drew closer together, closer than they had been in years. Most everyone in his life has shown him unconditional love. He has been fortunate.

He later told me, "I didn't realize it at the time but my hiding had also been the root cause of family tensions and some messed-up relationships with loved ones." It is important to remember that we have a responsibility to ourselves. If we are not healthy inside and don't give ourselves the respect that we deserve, we can never really share ourselves with anyone. Coming out may have caused some people in David's life pain at first, but it would have been worth it for David's sanity and the relationships that his honesty fostered in the long run.

Today David lives with his life partner. They've exchanged vows and experience the usual ups and downs as any straight couple might. And they are happy. David is living proof that we are rewarded when we trust in the ability of others to see with their hearts.

· EXERCISES ·

Six steps to feeling loved and fearless
1. Find a special place to go alone.
2. Spend fifteen minutes there each day.
3. Always go to the same place—make sure you're comfortable there.

4. Think only about you: your value as a human being, your right to be, you right to be loved.
5. Keep all problems and worries away.
6. Imagine being surrounded by those whom you love and ask them for their love—imagine a group hug!

This exercise will help you get in touch with your sense of self and the idea of inviting others in and trusting them. You will create a safe place that you will be able to escape to in your mind at any time. And after a few weeks have passed, you should feel more comfortable reaching out to others.

• • • •

Turning on the trust

This is a great exercise to help you get in touch with what you want others to see and what you're really like deep down in side. Take the insights about yourself gained from the first exercise and expand on them. Then ask yourself pointed questions and write them down. You might ask:

1. How do I work?
2. How do I handle responsibilities?
3. How do I communicate?
4. How do I deal with problems?
5. How do I relate to friends?
6. How do I handle pain?

Now, make a list with two columns. In the first column write, "How I want to be seen." In the second write, "How I really am."

After you complete this exercise, you will learn a lot about how you view yourself and it will help you overcome your fear of openness and being known. Just imagine anyone else filling out this same chart. We all have things that we like to keep to ourselves or a perhaps a certain image that we try to project. However, when we let that stop us from living, we get into trouble. This exercise will enable you to take a risk and trust in the ability of others to see you with their hearts.

CHAPTER 5

When Enough Is Not Enough

· ·

Perestroika: The Act of Tearing Something Down and Putting It Back Together

The massive Pan Am jumbo jet began its descent after the long Atlantic crossing, its engines winding down to a dull moan. Slowly signs of life began to emerge on the plains below us and my father and I braced for our arrival in the Soviet Union. What would it be like? What would we find? Could my salvation really rest with these people, the subject of so much scorn and distrust in the U.S.? We had been invited by a quasi-governmental organization called the Soviet Peace Committee to try an experimental surgery for spinal cord injuries. The Cold War still raged in 1988, though a hint of a thaw was in the air, and as my plane drew closer to Moscow a volatile cocktail of apprehension, excitement, and optimism swirled inside of me.

The journey to Russia was by far the biggest adventure and risk that I had ever taken (other than my decision to get into a car with a drunk driver). In Boulder, I was a regular student and had developed close friendships with young men and women from all walks of life. These new friends inspired me. They taught me that it was okay, and smart, to let people in. To harness their love and support in my struggle against adversity. More importantly, in contrast to ubiquitous tragic nighttime news programs and foreboding parental warnings, I was shown repeatedly how good people can be. Because of my powerful experience, I was able to move forward into the unknown with confidence. I thought to myself, "There just might really be people halfway around the world who care deeply enough that a young American woman might walk again."

Despite my optimism, the Soviet Union was still our sworn enemy and a profoundly foreign place at that time. I may have been invited with the best of intentions, but the distrust ran deep between America and Russia, and I felt uneasy as the plane coasted in and we taxied towards the bleak terminal building. Buses and all manner of official-looking vehicles swarmed around the aircraft as we pulled into the gate. The sky was gray and the terminal a bulwark of Soviet architectural sensibility. I sensed a lack of optimism in the gloomy color-starved landscape.

As guests of the state, I expected the royal treatment upon arrival. But when the door opened, Mother Russia gave us a taste of her dark side. As the passengers deplaned, my father and I were met by two scary-looking men in trench coats and immediately segregated from everyone else. They wore scowls and looked as if they were carrying out military orders.

"Nice to meet you; I'm David Stone," my father said cheerily, offering his hand to one of the men and doing his best to be a friendly ambassador of the American people. He stood there in his Brooks Brother's suit jacket and power tie, smiling like a successful southern gentleman about to negotiate business deal. They said nothing, nodding their heads and indicating which direction we were supposed to go through grunts and gruff gesturing. Then we were suddenly separated from each other. My father was taken away by one of the men and I was escorted into a drab, filthy, white room. It had industrial linoleum tiles on the floor and asbestos tiles on the ceiling, the kind you might find in old schools. The place reeked of cheap tobacco.

"I'll be right back honey," my father said as he was carted away. I could tell he was trying to convince me and himself that everything was on the up and up, just like he had hidden his fears from me right after my accident and during my days in rehab.

I waited and waited. After what felt like a half hour I began to get very nervous. *Where was my father? What's going on here?* I thought warily. We were drawn into this odyssey because we were told by the people on the Soviet Peace Committee that the doctors and sciences here were more advanced than in the U.S. We were assured that the medical community in Russia was able to pursue research and treatments considered too controversial in America. Sitting in what felt like an interrogation room in Sheremetyevo airport, with its *Dr. No*-era design elements, my first impression was of an economy under duress. The place was falling apart. It made me wonder if we had been duped by the infamous Soviet propaganda machine.

Finally a man with pursed lips came into the room and asked me for my passport in very stern, broken English. He must have seen the concern on my face because as I handed my documents over to him I was told, in a thick accent, "This is how we do arrival. Please no worry." But he was all business and offered no reassuring smile as he took my passport from me and marched off into an adjacent room. To my relief, moments later my father returned and I received my first glimmer of hope. A sign that everything might be okay after all. Standing next to him was a petite young woman with a welcoming Russian smile. Her name was Marina, our translator.

Our passports were returned safely and Marina ushered us through the security area. I recognized people from the plane waiting in line to pass through the fluorescent customs booth and be granted entry. As we whisked by with our official entourage, a man who had been sitting near us on the plane wished me luck. I had a feeling that I was going to need it. We were led outside into the brisk Russian morning where two Volgas, the Russians' take on Volvos, sat waiting for us. The adventure had begun.

A Strange Whole

Moscow was a city of contrasts. On the one hand it was a great European capital with incredible monuments from bygone eras. There were amazing old churches with shiny golden domes. The Kremlin and Red Square were absolutely beautiful. Graceful road-ways meandered along the Moscow River. The old architecture of the tsars was elegant and impressive. But then there were the stark edifices of the Soviet era: long, depressing buildings whose austere designs gave them a heaviness that was overpowering. This was the capital of the Soviet Union, and unlike Washington, D.C., whose broad boulevards and ebullient architecture convey a sense of optimism and pride, the structures of the Soviet era spoke of a large and all-powerful state that existed to control and dominate. It was as if two personalities lived side by side, very much like the gruff men who drove our car and delicate Marina. Two halves that comprised a very strange whole.

Thankfully, Marina seemed genuinely excited about being assigned to us and proud to show us her country's capital, pointing out different sights as we drove through the city. "Red Square, the Bolshoi," she said, pointing here and there, dealing out landmarks like a deck of playing cards. We were taken to the Hotel Ukraina, one of the so called "seven ugly sisters" from the Stalin era. The hotel is a thirty-story anomaly. The building slowly builds itself up in tiers like a rocket on a launch pad. A huge spire protrudes from the top. To be honest, the Hotel Ukraina looked to me like an enormous phallic symbol, and from what I know about Joseph Stalin I'm not surprised that he built such a monstrosity. I have heard that it has been renovated since my stay, but back in 1988 it was a poignant symbol of the deterioration of the communist system. The room was stale and, seeing hair wires here and there, we were quite sure that it was bugged. Supposedly modern, the elevator was cramped and dilapidated and I required the assistance of an operator to help me in and out of it. I couldn't help thinking that we were surrounded by basic machines that didn't work and yet I was planning to let them open my back and tamper with my already compromised spinal cord!

"Keep your eye on the prize honey," my dad told me in a voice meant to give me strength as he unpacked our things. "It's really not so bad. Things just need a facelift, that's all."

But we hadn't seen anything yet.

Hope

I was eager to delve into the purpose of our trip and come face to face with the people that we believed might cure me. Now for a bit of science.

The human spine is divided into three sections: the cervical section at the top where the head is attached, the thoracic section in the middle of the back, and the lumbar section at the bottom. I broke my back where the thoracic (middle) section meets the lumbar (lower) section, at what's called T-12 and L-1. The damage to the spinal cord causes the paralysis, not the break to the spine.

At the time of my injury, doctors described me as "incomplete," meaning I had not completely severed the cord and there was hope of my recovering some movement or sensation. At that point, spinal cord patients enter the six-month waiting room, a six-month period that determines whether you will spend the rest of your life sitting down or walking. Hope diminishes if you haven't regained substantial movement six months after the injury. I had not regained anything, and as a result had graduated to "complete" status, which meant, in layman's terms, that I was a hopeless case and any cure would amount to a miracle. A cure unknown to science then and now. It is important to understand that the peripheral nervous system heals itself. If you were to cut your finger off, you could sew it back on and it would function exactly or almost as it did before the accident. The central nervous system doesn't work that way. Once the damage is done, you're done. Enter stem cell therapy.

Stem cell therapy was not on the front pages back in 1988, as it is today. But right from the get-go, it was mired in controversy due to the source of the cells: human fetuses. At the time, they couldn't be grown in a lab and harvesting the cells from lost or aborted fetuses was the only option. Russia had taken a very sober approach to the science and pursued practical usages with vigor. I am sure that their passion came from the obsessive Soviet desire to outperform other societies. However, I am also just as sure that the people behind the research knew that if successful, their medical advances would revolutionize the treatments for various devastating diseases and conditions. What they wanted to do with me was place a bundle of fetal spinal cord tissue in the break in my spine. In theory, the cells would grow and create a bridge through which impulses could once again travel, turning the lower half of my body back "on," so to speak. Beyond my condition, stem cells were and are seen as the best hope we have for treating horrible diseases such as cancer, Parkinson's disease, and multiple sclerosis to name a few.

The next morning, we rose with difficulty due to severe jetlag and prepared to meet my destiny. In silence, my father and I gathered my things together and packed a small suitcase. It was really happening. I was going to meet people who thought that they could cure me. My father put on a tie and I dressed up as well. As luck would have it, the sun was shining. It was dreamy, that day. We were in a foreign land, completely out of sorts, and we both had the feeling that we were going to an interview by an admissions committee of some kind: would they find us worthy of their resources? Besides wanting to show the doctors respect, we were conscious of the fact that everyone was watching us. In 1988, Americans were an oddity in Russia and we were regarded as celebrities. In their eyes I could see both suspicion and simple curiosity.

Marina drove with us to the hospital. "Here it is, Hospital Number 67. It is the best in Moscow," she said as we pulled up to another drab Soviet rectangle. I was filled with excitement and apprehension. My father was quietly taking it all in with a serious look on his face and I could tell that he was assessing the facility in his head. Could this place hold the key to my being able to walk again? We entered the property through the back, through what seemed at first to be a beautiful courtyard. But the space quickly lost its charm when I saw the multitude of patients using the area for cigarette breaks and an opportunity to commiserate with one another. I didn't speak a word of Russian, but I could understand through their raised voices and shaking heads that those patients were miserable in Hospital Number 67.

When we stepped into the hospital my heart sank. To my American eyes, the building's condition was shocking. Its drab outside was vibrant compared to the dingy interior halls. I could have handled bleak sterility, but this was the most dilapidated hospital I had ever seen. It looked like a relic from WWII and felt totally unsanitary. I couldn't imagine anyone wanting to get blood drawn there, let alone have spinal surgery. I felt like joining the other patients in the courtyard for a comfort smoke. But Marina, all smiles, introduced us to the hospital administrator who was clearly proud to have an American among his patients as he escorted us to my room. I think Marina could tell that I was concerned because she leaned over and offered words of comfort. "Don't worry Carlana.

Everything will be fine. Best hospital and best doctors. Private room. Very nice. You will see."

We were escorted to my room, the only private room in the hospital. Everything looked filthy as we strolled down the halls. But by the time we got there, we were pleased enough. The room was, as Marina had promised, private. It lacked the high-tech gizmos of its Western counterparts, even a phone, but it was far better than the solitary-confinement-like stalls afforded the other patients. There was one single bed for me and the hospital had provided a bench for my father to sleep on. It was stored under the bed. Marina beamed, seemingly unaware of the chipping paint and hideous yellow color, and clearly confident that she and the Russian state had provided well for their American guests.

My dad and I stayed close and tried to get our bearings. Marina never left our side and I found myself taking a liking to her. She was my window on Russia. The first few days were filled with so many shocks and her happy face was reassuring.

Even fulfilling the most basic of needs turned into treacherous adventures that usually provided us with unwanted cross-cultural enlightenment. When, on the first day, I had to use the restroom, I was directed to a door about mid-way down the hall. Peering in, I was horrified to find what looked like a filthy hole in the ground. I know now that many other countries enjoy the ergonomics of the squat toilet, but it was a rude eye-opener in what had been a day of major culture shock.

The next morning they brought me breakfast. Two portly Russian women with disheveled hair came by pushing a metal cart bearing a large vat filled with sticky, lukewarm oatmeal. In addition to cement-like porridge, their cart of culinary delights offered a rotting apple and an egg, which wasn't boiled. Marina hadn't arrived and we tried to explain to them that our egg was raw. They were totally nonplused by our concern and we eventually deciphered that there was a kitchen down the hall where my father could boil the egg for me. We quickly came to understand that in Russian hospitals, it was the duty of the family to care for the patients. While there were nurses around, the family was responsible for their own. My poor father lost thirty pounds in the seven weeks he was there.

There was one bathroom on the floor with a communal tub, which had to be reserved. The water was cold, of course, and the hospital supplied no towels. I remember using a pillowcase to dry off. No one told us to bring towels. My father went to the American embassy trying to find someone who could help us. He wanted to hire someone to help take care of me, but the times being what they were he was finally told by one of the female attachés, "Why don't you get one of your friends from the Soviet Peace Committee to help you?" It seemed America felt that my family had made a deal with the devil.

Luckily, there were several people who emerged as allies during my stay. One person in particular was a medical student named Anatoly. My case was well known in the Moscow medical community and he was very interested in it. He was a sweet young guy, and by just making do with what little English he knew (and Marina's translation), we became friends. He understood the hard time that my father and I were having communicating, and on one of his visits he brought me an English-Russian dictionary. It was a small yet precious gesture. He visited me often and liked to talk about life and how we made our own destinies. Whenever he saw me his face would light up. I grew to look forward to his visits.

Finally it was time to meet the doctors. I remember vividly Marina and my father standing by my side when the doctors came to my room. There were three of them and Marina did all the translating. I was so nervous. Everything that I had seen so far had left me questioning the entire trip. But the moment that those three souls entered my room I was consoled. Like anyone trying to overcome adversity, I needed more than science that day. I need to feel their passion and confidence, two emotions which are beyond the scope of any translator.

The doctors explained through Marina what they were going to do. My father asked so many questions and we both felt frustrated by not being able to communicate with them directly. Yet, at the same time, I felt a sense of calm. As they spoke, I could see a fire in their eyes. I could sense their desire to help me walk again and I could feel their confidence. It was obvious that they cared very deeply about the work they were doing and believed in its efficacy. I trusted their eyes. They believed...they believed! And that's why I was there. For the first time since arriving, I believed too.

Fighting Against Negation

The day of the surgery had finally arrived. They were going to open up my back, prep the area around my damaged spinal cord to receive the stem cells, and then inject the first batch of cells.

On the day of the surgery, my Mom called in a desperate eleventh hour plea to postpone everything. She wanted to come, but we figured it would just be logistically easier for one parent to stay home in case we ran into trouble and needed help from outside of Russia. She had been trying to reach me for days, but the hospital, supposedly the best in Moscow, only had one phone and as a result she could never get through.

"Please honey, don't do this!" she cried into to the phone, her voice coated in static. She was frantic over the idea that I was putting myself in a dangerous situation given the general state of decay we'd reported seeing since our arrival in Moscow. But it was too late, I was now in another dimension and her reasoning couldn't reach me. I hated to know that she was suffering, but I just had to try. I had seen the doctors' eyes. I had tasted hope and I couldn't walk away.

Two attendants came to get me. They put me on a gurney and wheeled me down the hall. I was shaken by my mother's plea and my father had a strained look on his face. They had no drugs to spare and, unlike in the U.S., did not sedate me to help calm my nerves. I was wearing a brightly colored terry cloth robe, which made me stand out in my drab surroundings. I was like a dollop of color in a black and white film.

They rolled me to the end of the hall and stopped outside of the waiting room. At this point the two men reached around me and took off my robe, revealing my naked body for all to see, including my dad. I was horrified. But the Russians aren't tainted by our American prudishness. Nudity was perfectly natural to them. When they finally took me into the operating room my father broke down. He wanted to come with me so badly. Now his baby girl was in the hands of men who didn't speak a word of English and he would have to wait. It would be ten hours before we saw each other again.

In the operating room, I was alone with my Russian medical team. *My angels,* I thought. I couldn't believe what was about to happen. I thought about my mom and my sisters. I said a little prayer. And then they administered the anesthesia and everything went black. I drifted into a place somewhere between life and death. Suddenly, I was aware of being face down on a table. I could hear voices, and felt someone tugging at my back. They hadn't used enough anesthesia and it was wearing off. I started to panic and gasped for breath. I wanted to let them know that I was coming to but before I knew it I awoke in my hospital bed.

My father returned to the room shortly thereafter smelling of vodka. He had just returned from a victory "tea" with my two doctors Morosov and Alyoshin. They toasted with glasses of vodka and plates of vegetables and bread.

"Nellivai! To the success of your daughter's surgery!" they chimed victoriously. My father wasn't a big alcohol consumer but he couldn't refuse of course. The vodka was probably a welcome sedative for what had been one of his most stressful days.

It may have been the flood of hope that I was experiencing, but I was taken by the excitement that the doctors and nurses felt about me and my surgery. They didn't have much to offer, but they made up for their lack of tangible goods with an enthusiasm and happiness that stood out in stark juxtaposition to the world around them. They were filled with joy.

The surgery was really the first step in what would be ten days of painful stem-cell treatment. Every other day, I would be ushered into a dank room where doctors would inject stem cells into my spine with a twelve inch needle. If you're cringing, you should be. I didn't care though. This was where I would prove that I was worthy of the opportunity that I was given. I was at my best when I was fighting and working towards a goal. I went to Moscow because I had a dream to walk again, to dance again, to be whole again. I went in search of "the cure," and I was going to do everything possible to ensure that I found it.

As in rehab in Dallas, I began making friends with other patients. They were all spinal cord patients on my hall, or *invalidi* as the Russians called them. How I hated that word. In Russia, people in wheelchairs are not expected to be out and about and mixing with the able-bodied population. If paralysis strikes you, your life is over as you know it. You're a shut-in. You literally either live holed up in an upper floor apartment and rarely leave your house or you go to live in a *sanitorium*. Society basically has no need for you and certainly no means to accommodate you. When you're an "invalid" you have absolutely nothing to offer and are a drain on everyone; the state, your family, the government, strangers, and passersby.

I think that it is more than that. I think that when people see paraplegics or quadriplegics, they evoke feelings of fragility that they spend most of their lives running from. It's almost too painful for people to be in your presence because they don't want to recognize or even acknowledge all the pain that exists in the world or inside of themselves. That was why people looked at me with a combination of fascination and shock when I wheeled around my hotel and on the streets of Moscow. The people on my floor were trying to fight against their negation. They were filled with a powerful spirit and drive to stay relevant, something with which I identified completely.

In speaking with my fellow patients, I realized that I had been placed on a pedestal. Contrary to reviling me because I was American, my nationality made me a star. I was treated like, well, Miss America. Everyone wanted to be with me and seemed eager to ask questions about life in my homeland. They were so demanding of my attention that I felt like I was on display everywhere I went. I loved it. It was perfect medicine for me. I was in a place where I was an instant star. Ironically, despite my physical condition, people were drawn to me like a ray of hope in their faltering, gray environment.

The fascination was not one sided. I was beginning to understand and appreciate Russia. While it is true that there was a great deal of suffering, it was also a very soulful place that was equally caring as it was harsh—two halves of a very strange whole.

As I healed from my surgery, I worked hard and tried to will my body to accept the new tissue and heal. My father and I stayed in Moscow for seven weeks. As in Boulder, my room became a busy place, with people coming and going. It seemed that everyone had taken a personal interest in my case and was eager to see me succeed. My doctors would come by every day to check on me and ask about progress, walking into my room with happy faces and a friendly, "Hello, Carlana!" They really believed in what they were doing and that I would walk again. More than that, they really wanted it to happen for me.

During my stay, I was introduced to Valentine Ivanovich Dikool. He was a former strongman of the Moscow circus and a member of the politburo. He was injured when he fell from a tightrope and broke his back. He was paralyzed, but rehabilitated himself and was able to walk just as he did before the accident. In his spare time, he lifted cars in the circus to boast his strength but he was also a major force behind a rehab in Moscow. He employed the philosophy that is hypnotic to people without hope: "If I can do it you can too." And nobody, I mean nobody, questioned him. His dream was to take those of us who were told we would never walk again and destroy the word "never." He invited me to stay in Russia and find salvation at the rehab. I couldn't, though I wanted to.

The seven weeks flew by and soon I found myself having to say goodbye to the team of people that had dedicated themselves to my quest for the cure. It was an emotional day at the hospital. Everyone had shown me so much kindness and inspired me to reach for the cure. The Russian people had revealed themselves to be caring and open, not citizens of some evil empire. Perhaps because they had so little and struggled so much, I connected with them on a very basic level. Despite being able to conduct innovative scientific research on shoestring, their country was a mess. It was apparent that the USSR was faltering. Like me, they had lost important resources. Many tangible symbols of success and happiness had been stripped from them. But they found joy in each other. They held on to hope. Looking in from the outside, it seemed to me that their chief assets were their pride, conviction, and warmth and that international politics had distorted their true identity.

The day I left the hospital, a nurse gave me a note from Anatoly, my friend the medical student. It was written in Russian and on the plane I had a flight attendant translate the letter.

Dear Carlana,

It is a great pity to me that I was not able to see you off. But in spite of that I am with you and I want to tell you a few words in parting.

I believe that you will rise without fail. You will rise! You will rise despite all! And my faith in that is not lacking in foundation, since we medical people are to some degree realists. You are the first person in whom I have encountered that quality for which there is no name. Without it one can live but cannot rise. But for you to rise is simply unavoidable and you will rise!

Such people as you, little one, must stand. You will rise because even in an invalid's chair, life cannot place you on your knees.

I thank fate for meeting you.
Anatoly

Reading Anatoly's heartfelt letter empowered me. I thought of my doctors, of all the wonderful people that I had met. "You will rise." Anatoly was a wise man and understood what I did not at that young age: that my cure, *rising*, might not mean standing at all.

Stubborn Progress

I returned to the U.S. hopeful that the treatments I received in Russia would slowly bring about a transformation in my condition. They provided me with a series of stretching exercises that

I was to perform every day in order to keep my body healthy and encourage, I suppose, the stem cells to settle into their new home and start passing messages on to my legs.

After spending a semester away, I returned to Boulder a much more sober student. I still did my fair share of bar hopping, but I wasn't putting my social life first any longer. I felt that I had a duty to my father and mother, the doctors in Russia, and myself to do everything I could to ensure that the therapy worked. I allowed myself to believe that I might actually be cured, a dangerous freedom for a paraplegic because it meant that I was setting myself up for potential heartache.

In discussing my trip and surgery, I was surprised to find that many people were shocked that I risked being operated on in a strange country. Most said that they would have listened to the American doctors if they told them that there was no hope. Still others balked at putting themselves in the hands of the Russians, a shadowy people back in 1988. When I told people about the dilapidated nature of the hospital, most said that they would have turned tail and taken the next flight home. I couldn't believe the response. I needed to feel confident that I had tried everything before I gave into my bleak diagnosis. I had to exhaust all my options before I gave up hope of ever walking again.

After I was home for about six months, I went in for a consultation with a doctor at the Miami Project to Cure Paralysis, a top-notch research group in Miami, Florida, dedicated to treating spinal-cord injuries. I hadn't experienced any miracle moment, not even one baby step, and was told that the surgery was a failure.

Still, I refused to give in. I had tasted hope in Russia and reasoned that I just wasn't trying hard enough. I felt that I needed to make my search for the cure the central focus of my life and to be in a place that would encourage me to push on, even when everyone else told me that I had reached the end of the road.

Eventually my thoughts led me back to Valentine Ivanovich Dikool, the man with the conviction, the guts, to heal. I decided right then and there that I would get myself back to Russia as soon as possible so that I could continue my quest for the cure.

Lesson Learned: *You Are Entitled to a Say in Your Own Destiny*

Overcoming any adversity is difficult. It is especially hard when someone is telling us that our options are limited and, in essence, to resign ourselves to our fate.

Sometimes the situation is indeed as grave as everyone is telling us. Many people who knew my case told me to forget about walking again and just accept my condition. Perhaps this advice was offered in my best interest. They didn't want to see another person chase after pipedreams just to end in heartache and disappointment. It sounds rational.

The issue I have is that sometimes we need to make our own mistakes. Sometimes the rational approach doesn't mesh with our human condition. For our own peace of mind, it is important that we keep pushing against all odds. There is always the chance of a spectacular result: a miracle. However, even if there is no pot of gold at the end of the rainbow, or all our efforts are for naught, at least we can move forward and know that we tried. And this helps us feel that we are not victims. It gives us a sense of empowerment because we are able to take, even if just in spirit, the power back from our circumstance. When someone tells you to give in and you do not feel ready to, listen to your heart and,

SEE IT THROUGH

Let people say that you're wasting your time. Let them scoff at you. But know that in the end you will feel that it was you and not an accident or a doctor that decided it was time to embrace a new path.

Living Proof: *Survivor*

A coworker of mine, let's call her Sharon, came to me a few years ago when she found out she had breast cancer. Sharon's had cancer not once but twice. She experienced a recurrence four years after her initial diagnosis at the age of thirty-eight. Needless to say, she was scared.

Sharon had to have a mastectomy followed by extensive radiotherapy. Luckily, she had a few months of sick leave with half-pay. She was single, and being left in the hospital for her mastectomy, she recalls, was the most miserable day in her life. She told me that she whimpered for hours about losing her femininity. Sharon was a salsa dancer in her free-time and, just like me when I was a young gymnast, so much of her identity was based on her physical appearance. She feared that she had lost her sexuality forever.

After the surgery, when she saw her body for the first time, she was shattered and in shock and felt like her life was ruined. She was also angry, as she always considered herself a healthy individual and questioned how something so tragic could happen to her.

Even though her doctor told her she was cured, she questioned his positive attitude. Apathy set in and she stopped caring about the things that normally gave her joy. Sharon wouldn't buy clothes because she felt like it was a waste of money; she reasoned that she would probably die soon—what was the point?

During the period immediately following her surgery and her follow-up treatments, she often came to me. She was so down and felt like giving up. Sharon told me how much she hated seeing herself in the mirror and how she felt ashamed of her altered body. Even though she started to see a therapist to help her through her feelings, she didn't think that there could ever be another bright day.

I told her to keep going. I told her that I understood and had been down a similar road. I told her that no matter what, she needed to keep pushing herself forward because one day she would find joy again. It was hard for her to imagine that she would ever feel comfortable in her body, but there I was, a paraplegic, driving around and living a full life, evidence that it was possible to overcome a great physical loss. I made her promise to follow through with all her therapies and to seek additional therapy through groups and other social activities if she felt her needs weren't being met.

I also made her think of her healing as a process that involved more than skin and soft tissue. She needed to take the experience and use it as a lens through which to see the world. She needed to address all of the feelings that she was having as well as the physical suffering and see them both through to a new life. That way, I told her, she would feel that she had done all she possibly could to heal herself and take control of her situation.

"No one knows what's going to happen in the future, but there's a certain peace of mind that comes from knowing we did our best. That we took a proactive role in our lives," I told her. She listened and said that she would try.

It was only after the radiotherapy was over that she could start to resume somewhat normal activities. Although she herself was not yet up to dancing, some evenings she would push herself to go out and watch other people dance. Over time, the music and the energy of the people began to soothe her. Even though she wasn't ready to join them, it gave her something to look forward to. Slowly but surely, she wanted to "rejoin the living," so to speak.

Sharon was also someone who, before the second bout with cancer, kept her feelings well hidden. She was uncomfortable telling people how she felt about them, even family members. But not any more. As she made her way through the healing process, she recognized that she needed to change her behavior. She began to reach out. She realized that sharing her feelings gave her peace and also relieved stress. She even felt less alone. Sharon began to realize that she could determine how far her healing went and how fast, in some ways, she would get there. She pushed ahead.

Today, Sharon is more connected with the people in her life than she's ever been. She makes sure that her family and friends know how special they are to her. She also lets them know when she's unhappy about something they've done. On a more basic level, she always takes time to smell the roses and finds something good in each day.

As part of her healing, she has also made sure that her friends learned from her experience. She has encouraged her female friends to have annual mammograms and checkups. She is open to questions and willing to discuss her experience. This has given her a sense of control over what was once an overpowering force in her life.

Today Sharon is cancer-free. Still, she knows that she can't predict the future. But she has a sense of awareness and an inner peace that has come from taking charge of her healing and, in so doing, her life. She has seen it through on all levels, emotional and physical.

Sharon is living proof that by not being complacent and taking an active role in overcoming seemingly un-winnable situations we can feel better about ourselves and our destinies. Stay the course and see it through, no matter what the outcome.

· EXERCISES ·

Pay no attention to boundaries

In overcoming my adversity, I have found it helpful to think that there are no boundaries in life. That life is what we make of it. I have found this philosophy, in most cases, to be true. If this works for me, it will work for you too!

Pick out any goal you want to accomplish and write it down. Your goal could be small or large. Write down a game plan, decide on a path, and explore the consequences. Then act. Think outside of the box, but be systematic and disciplined. Change your strategy if you need to along the way. But see it through! Go for it and stay the course. You will find that no matter what happens, whether you succeed or not, you will feel fulfilled and proud because you fully invested yourself in something that you believed in. You will feel in greater control of your life. This is a great way to build your confidence. Work towards small goals and then towards larger ones.

My Goal:

The Consequences:

The Path: (steps)

My Action: (what, when, where)

1. Become aware of your intentions
2. Consider the impact of each of your intentions.
3. Choose the intention that will create the consequences you desire (this is a responsible choice).
4. Observe how your experiences change.
5. If your experiences do not change, ask yourself which parts of your personality are holding you back.
6. Address them and think about what you can do to change them.
7. Do the experiment again.

CHAPTER 6

The Power of Perspective

• •

My Personal Rasputin

I had never totally given up on a cure. Even when I was told that my injury was permanent, I kept my eyes open for someone who offered a way back. Someone who wouldn't tell me to accept life in the chair as all the American doctors had. I searched for the man or woman who would look me in the eye and say, "You can walk again. You can dance. If you just do as I say." Valentine Ivanovich Dikool was that man.

I returned to the Soviet Union in war mode. It had been almost a year since the surgery, and while I was able to discern things like hot or cold against my skin I still couldn't walk or even stand. I was disappointed and frustrated because I felt that if medical researchers in my country were allowed to explore the science, things might have turned out differently. There is no telling where we would be today if gifted and well funded American scientists had been able to take a leading role in the research.

Recently the people of California voted in favor of Proposition 71, which dedicated three billion dollars in state funding to embryonic stem cell research. Amazingly, this makes California the leading researcher of stem cells in the U.S., public or private. The reason Prop. 71 passed is that beyond spinal injuries, stem cells are widely seen as potential treatments for chronic and devastating diseases such as Parkinson's, Alzheimer's, multiple sclerosis, cancer, and even heart disease. Nearly sixteen years after my surgery, young researchers in California are using embryonic stem cells to make paralyzed rats walk again.

All the brilliant minds advocating the research can't be wrong and I am hopeful that we are our way to discovering effective treatments. But back in 1989, like today, I was forced to look beyond science to pure will and gumption for my cure. I was ready to submit totally to Dikool and do whatever it took to maximize the benefits of my surgery and get back on my feet.

It had taken some diplomatic and financial wrangling to work out all the details, but I arranged to stay in a hotel near the rehab run by Dikool. He had agreed to take me on out of a deep sentimental commitment to helping the helpless and a new-found fondness for the American greenback. No one had any idea that he was a harbinger of times to come.

I had no friends (other than the acquaintances that I made during my first stay), no family, and no language ability. But I did have *hope*. I also had hard currency and contacts in high places, something useful to a twenty-year-old American woman living alone in the deteriorating capital of political intrigue. When I came to Moscow the first time, I literally envisioned getting off the operating table and walking away. I had the same vision when

I returned to Russia for physical therapy under the almost mystical guidance of Valentine Dikool. I went back to Russia daring to believe that dreams can come true.

There was no fanfare this time. The state was happy to have me but they weren't going to roll out the red carpet. They couldn't afford to do so if they wanted to. Upon arrival, I was brought to the hotel Zvezdnaya. Whereas the Hotel Ukraina stood as a proud phallus over the Moscow skyline, the hotel Zvezdnaya was a practical Soviet cement rectangle about ten stories tall. Floodlights along the roofline illuminated its name like a beacon of hope to weary travelers, who, upon arrival, invariably felt like victims of false advertising. The place lacked any optimism whatsoever. It was as bleak as the gray Moscow winter sky.

Several other patients from Dikool's rehab were also interned at the hotel Zvezdnaya. They hailed from cities across the Soviet Union. Some were almost as far away from home as I was. My room was spacious enough, though it was bare and dated. I hoped the hotel Zvezdnaya would be half as good to me as Libby Hall had been.

Since the hotel offered little in terms of food, one of the medical students that used to visit me during my first stay in Moscow helped me settle in. He took me to a Russian grocery store for some supplies. It was the first time that I had a glimpse into the mundane aspects of Russian life and it was surreal to say the least. The store had long aisles just like in the U.S., but the shelves were literally empty. There were a few boxes of kasha on one shelf, but nothing more. My friend said, "We will have to come back another day, hopefully then, the government will replenish some supplies." We tried a few days later and found that frozen chickens had been added to the menu. The Muscovites called them "Bush Legs" because the country had received the chickens as a gift from America (The Bush family has such a proud legacy when it comes to foreign affairs).

My program at the rehab commenced almost immediately. The other patients and I would wake up every morning and board a diesel-powered bus that was sent especially for us. On my first day, I remember smiling optimistically at everyone and wishing people good morning out of habit. I felt like it was the first day of school. But my fellow patients looked at me with sober faces that reminded me of miners about to descend for hours of subterranean hard labor. Once we arrived at the rehab and I started my therapy, I understood why. It was clear that the University of Dikool was not going to be a walk in the park.

"Carlana, you are here. Good!" Dikool said firmly when I arrived at the center. "You will see, so many people working hard. It will come back! Understand?" he asked me. There was only one possible answer.

"Yes. That's why I'm here," I said with a smile.

"Good!" he barked. He was a huge grizzly bear of a man. He had the stern presence of a general addressing one his soldiers. Nobody, paying patients and employees alike, ever questioned Valentine Ivanovich Dikool. If he said I could walk again, it would be so. He was beyond question and able to bend fate. He was my very own personal Rasputin.

I Am Wealthy

Like my old hospital room, the rehab was a shabby place. Paint peeled from the cement walls like bark from a birch tree. There were about a dozen or so aluminum exercise stations designed by Dikool. It was clean, however, and there were mirrors running the length of each wall, which created the illusion of a vast Orwellian landscape populated by Dikool's strange machines. Though it was rather grim, some light managed to peek through the row of windows that topped a wall at the end of the gym. I could never understand the lack of light in their buildings. It was as if the Russians were reveling in their despair by maximizing their solar deprivation.

On my first day, I was introduced to Tatiana Stepanovana. Tatiana was to be my personal exercise therapist. She was a short, brown-haired woman in her mid forties and wore bright pink lipstick and rouge. I sensed her goodness instantly. Gina back in Boulder would have loved the challenge.

"Hallo," She offered by way of a greeting. I would learn that it was the only English word she knew. She smiled, revealing several gold teeth that glinted under the fluorescent lighting, and then quickly shut her mouth, clearly self-conscious of her ore-rich smile.

I was then introduced to my stretching therapist Saroja Evgenovich Chugayev, or simply Saroja, as he was known. He was hands down the best looking man I had ever seen. With his Baryshnikov-esque chiseled features, green eyes, and lanky, muscular form, he personified the Russian ideal of male beauty. Hell, he personified anyone's ideal of male beauty!

"*Preevyet,*" he said, Russian for hello, holding out his hand in a very businesslike manner. I could tell by the way that he held his head, tipped slight back and to the side, that he had a lot of pride. I had the feeling that in his mind he was saying, "You may be a rich American but you're just another patient to me." There was the faintest hint of a smirk running across his face.

"*Ochen Preeyatnuh!*" It's very nice to meet you, I said.

He rescinded his hand and folded his arms across his chest, allowing his smirk to reveal itself in full cocky form. This was not the kind of welcome that I was used to receiving in Russia. As the *Amerikansky Devushka*, the American girl, I was treated almost as a kind of royalty. Lots of men flirted with me and I was disappointed when Saroja didn't give me the time of day. Not surprisingly, I immediately became obsessed with him.

Therapy, like Dikool, was very rough. Each day, I spent several hours stretching, exercising, swimming, and hurting. The day would begin with Saroja. It was his job to try to stretch out my tight tendons. I hadn't tried to keep myself limber at all times, because in America I was told that there really was no hope. What was the point of stretching body parts that weren't ever going to be needed again?

The first day he took my leg and pushed my knee back to my chest I thought I was going to die. The only thing that kept me from screaming wildly was his beautiful face, which hung over me like a Russian dream. I didn't want to him to think I was weak, so I bit my lip and only let out a few gasps. He could tell that I was suffering, but he offered no olive branch, no tenderness, and instead, grimaced like a coach frustrated by an athlete not working up to her ability.

"Hey, I have other strengths. Look," I told him in English, flexing my arms to communicate my point. He waved his hand at me telling me, in perfectly clear and apparently universal sign language, to give him a break. He poked me on my arm and pointed across the room to Tatiana, who was instructing another patient on a machine.

"Tatiana," he said, puckering his lips, rolling his eyes, and blowing a silent whistle like a lovelorn adolescent. He completed his tease with a thumbs up sign. Then he pointed back at my legs and opened his arms like a priest on a pulpit chiding his flock for their lack of moral fiber.

Fucker, I thought. He was doing his best to get my goat and it was working. Little by little, though, he became very playful and I could tell that he wasn't totally immune to my American charms.

While Saroja was a sexy little devil, Tatiana was a Russian angel and her pink lips and fruity cheeks eventually became a comforting sight to me. She really cared about her patients and though we weren't able to speak with each other in our respective tongues, we somehow managed to communicate complex ideas with relative fluency. When I look back at my time with her, it is not fraught with memories of frustrating linguistic impasses. Instead, I remember our time together as one of bonding and full of meaningful exchanges.

Dikool's contraptions were designed to isolate muscles and maximize their usage. I had to wear metal boots which supported my ankles and forced my knees into a locked position, in essence overextending them. Those things would have allowed a scarecrow to walk on its own. I suppose, given their state of affairs, the Russians didn't care to think in terms of the future, choosing instead to focus on getting through the here and now. Perhaps this is a projection on my part. Either way, no one ever stopped to consider the permanent damage that occurred as a result of repeatedly overextending our knee joints. Despite the long-term effects, which would haunt me for years to come, each movement was sheer misery and made me feel like I was going to be snapped in half at the knee. But, not long after I arrived, I was walking with the aid of his devices and the eye-level perspective they afforded me was a welcome respite from the midriff doldrums to which I had grown so accustomed.

When I wasn't walking in braces I stood with cords connecting my waist or my legs to metal weights. I would lift them again and again. Over and over. Every day, day in and day out. It was grueling. In the beginning I would ride with my fellow invalidi back to our barracks where, after eating bad food at a local restaurant and drinking heavily in someone's room, I would cry myself to sleep. In therapy, I found that I couldn't stand up without my face flying into the bars of the torture devices designed by Dikool.

On top of that, Russia was so depressing. People were starving and it was sometimes hard to even look out of the bus window as we drove through the city on our way to the rehab. All the gaunt faces. Stick figure children in somber gray clothing clutching their mothers' boney hands. I was searching for a miracle in a place where the well of human spirit seemed to have run dry. All I saw in their eyes was an enormous sense of loss and apprehension about the future. There were many times when I contemplated getting on the phone with Pan Am and getting the hell out of there.

But pain or misery would not drive me away. In retrospect, I was probably stronger for them. In any case, if I had left early on, I would've felt like a failure, a quitter. Labels I feared more than *"invilidi"* or "cripple." People back home expected me to return triumphant, standing,...fixed. Once, I called my friend Sue from Moscow and while we were talking, I heard her mom in the background ask, "She walking yet?" My entire town was following me through the newspapers and all my friends had bought into the idea that Russia, a land cloaked in mystery, was the keeper of secret knowledge hidden deep behind its iron curtain.

I brought the photo album that my friends in Boulder gave me as a going away present. At night I would flip through it and draw strength from the knowledge that somewhere in the world, at that very moment, there were people who were sending me love and luck. I would imagine hands all around me, keeping me safe. And after some reflection, I would reaffirm my commitment to my cause and declare, like Scarlet O'Hara looking over the ruins of Tara, that I would never doubt myself again. That I would walk away from Russia or die trying. The cure was here. I just had to work hard enough to find it.

In spite our language barrier, I began to make inroads into Tatiana and Saroja's lives. Russians love tea and Tatiana would often break for tea and sweets with the other therapists. One day she invited me to come along. I was thrilled. It was the day that I learned my first Russian sentence, *"Chai gariachi? Ya hachoo peet chai!"* Is the tea hot? I'd like some tea. From that day forward, Tatiana doubled as my language tutor (until I employed a real one). Each day during my exercises she would teach me new words and phrases and within a few months of arriving I was able to hold rudimentary conversations. I suppose it was the constant practice that allowed me to pick things up so fast. A few years later American businessmen would pay thousands of dollars for the total-immersion Russian language programs that offered the same kind of experience. Besides making things easier on a pragmatic level, like ordering food or asking directions, I was able to impress Saroja with a new word every time he came to help me work out. Sometimes he would correct my pronunciation but other times he would smile and say, "Very good." In English. That's when I knew I was getting to him.

As the months passed Tatiana and I developed a certain intimacy that transcended the therapist-patient relationship. She would wail at me whenever I showed up for therapy with just a light shirt and a leather jacket, scolding me over and over again and warning me that I was going to catch pneumonia. When I finally did catch a cold, she showed up at my hotel room with a hotplate in hand, cooked me liver and onions, drew a hot bath, gave me a shot of vodka, and tucked me in bed. In many ways, Tatiana was like a mother to me. My little pink-lipped *Muscovite mama*.

She also became more and more committed to my progress. She cheered me on as I struggled though my exercises. I had moved halfway around the world to be there, but during those long, painful days, I often wanted to quit. I hadn't experienced any major transformation and still relied on the chair and my arms to get around. Tatiana could sense how unhappy I was in the chair and didn't allow me the option of giving up. I remember grunting my way through an exercise and just as I finished, so happy to be done with it, she would add another weight and push me further. I used to get angry and curse and she would stand there very patiently and let me have my little tantrums. Then she would start up all over again, and say, *"Divai*

Payekhali!" Let go. I told her about my crush on Saroja, and whenever I didn't work hard enough on my exercises or demanded that we stop, she threatened to reveal my secret to him.

One morning Tatiana was late. The food might not be in the shops when you needed it and the sun might decide not to show up for several days but Tatiana was never late. After about a half hour or so I went looking for her. I eventually found her in the women's locker room looking very upset and talking with another therapist, who was holding both her hands. I could tell that I had interrupted a private, and obviously difficult, moment so I quickly returned to the exercise room to wait for her.

When she came out to meet me her eyes were red and puffy and together with her bright pink rouge she looked like an elderly lady who just ducked out of a cold wind. There was an awkward moment of silence and then I couldn't help but ask what the matter was. At first she resisted and told me that she didn't want to burden me with her troubles. But I pried and she finally gave in. She told me that she had just returned form Dikool's office where she had asked for an advance in her pay. He had told her no. I immediately offered her money. I assumed that there was some emergency that needed to be addressed. She scoffed at my offer and flat out refused, almost scolding me and telling me never to offer her money again. She said that she would find a way out of her situation by herself. She was proud and didn't want any handouts.

Eventually more details emerged. Russia was poor, but it never occurred to me that skilled working people like Tatiana would be impacted so brutally by the collapsing state economy.

In Russia, people used government-issued food stamps to buy food. But the markets were empty. I mean bare. Even restaurants had to pare down their menus. America had donated those annoying frozen chickens, but it by no means met the vast need. And there was something depressing, even to hungry Muscovites, about walking into a supermarket with no food except for a freezer full of frozen chicken. The Russian people were literally starving, and the only immediate way out of hunger was to buy food on the black market, where the cost was five times the store prices. This was Tatiana's emergency. Her and her husband's monthly salaries were no longer enough to adequately feed themselves and their little boy.

The grave situation brought on a deluge of headhunting opportunists from foreign lands. Russia offered a vast pool of skilled workers who were willing to work at rock-bottom prices. They had even come to Dikool's center. Many had taken the offers, but Tatiana, of course, couldn't leave her family.

Despite the horrible backdrop of desperation and need, Tatiana continued to come to work everyday and focus on *me*. On *my* rehabilitation. This was her job and she relied on it as a matter of life and death, but I promise you there was no detached professionalism on her part. She continued to invite me for cups of tea, sometimes little more than tarnished hot water because the bag had been reused so many times, and she continued to smile.

Even after my Russian improved and our relationship deepened, I never saw her upset after that day. Sometime later I asked her how she was managing and she smiled and told me in Russian, "Nobody starves; son is healthy, husband healthy. I am wealthy." I noticed that she had lost weight, and when I pointed it out she looked at herself in the mirror, turned sideways and said, "Not bad, eh."

"Not bad," I said, wrapping my arms around her neck and giving her hug. "Not bad at all.

Lesson Learned: The Power of Perspective

I had arrived in Russia seeking a cure to paralysis. I wanted to be fixed. Normal. I felt fatally flawed and was convinced that I would never feel complete unless I was able to leave the wheelchair behind and walk again. The chair dominated my consciousness and as a result I was unable to appreciate my many riches. My cup, so to speak, always seemed half empty. And though I still couldn't walk, after all my hard work, Russia did offer a "cure." My experience there, bearing witness to the way Tatiana and others dealt with their adversity, gave me an incredible insight to the means by which I could transcend my paralysis. They showed me that I was fortunate in so many ways. They showed me that we are ultimately responsible for our own happiness and sense of well-being. I had a wealth of friendships and a loving family behind me. I was financially comfortable. I was loved. But, until my time in Russia, I couldn't really appreciate the true value of these things. I came to see that if my injury was a heavy darkness, those things were powerful sources of light.

Tatiana taught me that how well we cope with situations depends on how we process them. When times are tough, we can choose to obsess on the negative and in so doing miss out on the little things that give us joy. Or we can choose, (and the key word is *choose*; it is a *conscious* decision), to exploit the joy in our lives to its fullest and savor the happiness that is available to us. Sharing cups of tea, evenings with friends and family, pot-luck suppers, afternoons in the park—those are the kinds of things that got many Russians through very dark times. They sound simple and trite. But, it is often the simple things that give our life meaning.

I have a friend that likes to say, "It's the little things that'll kill you." I like to think that they can also save us during our time of need. Tatiana and her fellow Russians understood this and because of their insight I am sure they could handle most anything that came at them. This is the hallmark of a survivor: the ability to process what's happening so that it doesn't consume them. These are the immigrants who show up in a foreign land with nothing, often relegated to the edges of society, and in one generation own homes and businesses. The people who get fired and turn around and create their own successes. They all employ the following tool and you can too:

CHOOSE TO SEE THE GLASS HALF FULL

That is what I learned, what we all can learn, from the people in Russia and others like them. Over time, people that seemed beaten and exhausted when I arrived appeared resilient and deft in their ability to find strength in the world around them, in the people in their lives, and in the small pleasures still available to them. They opened my eyes to the truth that, even after all my hardships, I still had much to be grateful for and it was up to me to keep my worries in perspective.

Living Proof: *Losing a Job*

Ten years ago, Shelly was coming out of a divorce, raising three children, and struggling to make a living. Wanting a better way of life for herself and her family, she put herself through nursing school and graduated at the top of her class. The day she graduated was perhaps the proudest day of her life.

She began working immediately at her city's most prestigious hospital. She was older than most of the young girls just starting out. She became a mentor for them, offering them not only professional advice but also motherly advice. Everything was great until one day her world came crashing down. The hospital had to make some cutbacks and they decided to keep on the younger girls who were willing to work longer hours for less money. Shelly was devastated. Her job held a great deal of personal meaning. It wasn't just money, it was a reason for being that went beyond motherhood. And to Shelly, in a way, losing that identity was like a death.

Shelly told me that along with the loss of her identity came the loss of her financial means: "How am I supposed to care for my kids?" She had to find a way to survive without that monetary security. Feelings of betrayal, loss of trust, and disrespect remain. Shelly felt all alone and lost with nowhere to go. She searched aimlessly and unsuccessfully to find another job in the nursing field. What was she to do? She felt like she was at the end of her rope. Or was she?

When we are faced with adversity, sometimes our perspective is the only tool over which we have control. The world is full of high-profile success stories that have, at their root, a devastating dismissal. If you find yourself out of work, it is critical that you sit down and take stock of things that are right with your life. I had Shelly literally sit down and write down the things that give her life meaning. She felt consoled. I guarantee that you will too. If there is something tangible that you can point to on your most trying days, you will navigate them more easily and reach your goal, your salvation, more quickly. You will know where to turn, whether it be a friend, church, a museum or a beach, community centers, whatever, when you need help. Moreover, you will feel that your glass really is half full.

Incidentally, we need not be facing a specific struggle to benefit from a healthy acknowledgment of our blessings. Though the practice is critical during moments of great stress, I believe that it could benefit us all in our day to day lives. I have a list of friends, family, personal qualities, and other attributes that make my life rich. I am always aware of them and they are a constant source of strength for me. My cup truly runneth over. Like Tatiana, I feel wealthy every day.

Besides, if you have your list ready when times are good, you will be better prepared to face adversity should it strike. Shelly and I worked on a list for her. She started a daily ritual of recognizing the things which she had formerly taken for granted. Life isn't perfect for any of us, but our perspective can change the way we live it and our happiness.

Today, Shelly keeps her list close to her and it is a small yet strong pillar of support, a tangible reminder of all the good things she has to be thankful for. She has found part-time work as a freelancer in the emergency ward and remains optimistic about her future.

Shelly now recognizes the power of choice. Instead of stressing about the future, she embraces every opportunity to be with her kids, attending their ballgames and dance recitals. Shelly is living proof that life changes for the better when we choose to see the glass as half full.

· EXERCISES ·

Rut or furrow?

Are you in a rut or furrow? The rut is a ditch that goes on and on....the furrow is like a farmer plowing ; the dirt is continually turning over. In chapters 4 and 5, you read that in order to get out of the rut and onto a furrow you have to take risks. We're all looking for happiness.

For this exercise, gather some small rocks that are big enough for you to write on. Take out a pen and on each rock write a rut that you have experienced. When you have written on enough rocks to fill a clear vase, put them in the vase. When you look at that vase full of ruts, it seems there is no way out.

If you have access to some sand, that's best, but some rice will do. Think of the way you are not living up to your potential. Think of what you can do to better yourself. Think of some life changes you can make. With each of those thoughts, put a spoonful of sand or rice into that vase of rocks. Before you know it, you will fill in all of those crevices and be able to visualize your potential for happiness, not forgetting the ruts, but budding happiness all around them. And there's plenty of room! If you don't believe me, after you have filled the vase with rocks and sand, add some water that is labeled "extra happiness experiences." Your cup runneth over! As does your life.

. . . .

Losing a job is awful— but it can help you find your true calling.

Losing a job can wipe you out emotionally. If you find yourself out of a job, there are some proactive steps to take. Write down how you feel each day for two weeks after losing your job. Continue each day charting your frustration, your sorrow, your sense of loss, confusion, anger, etc. Write each day until you feel emptied. Just this exercise alone will help you overcome some of the "post-traumatic" stress that you're bound to feel after losing a job. It will help you begin to heal and stop feeling like a victim. Also, form or join a support group. Link up with others in your same situation. Talk about what happened, how you felt; talk about what you miss, what you don't miss. Name something you will always be proud of from your last job. Brainstorm with everyone about how to find a new job. There is power in numbers and you feel less alone and grief-stricken if you give yourself a chance to get it all out. With the help of others and some soul-searching, you can find your calling and path to indestructible happiness—the true measure of success.

CHAPTER 7

Learning to Listen to Your Soul

A Change in Focus

The days lengthened and the delicate Russian spring finally made its way up to Moscow. It couldn't have come sooner. Things were just too lean, literally, to cope with another gray month. Russian people have a friendly understanding with winter; they bitch and moan like everybody else but they never complain too much. Their winter has saved them from foreign threats many times and they tolerate it like a bellicose old ally, much like France and the United States. But not that year. The winter of 1990 was another story all together. That winter left them feeling sequestered from a world that was beating them on every front. They were stuck in a war of ideology that was beyond the reach of the brutal polar winds that swept down across the great steppes. And in April of that year, on the few days when the temperature dipped below freezing, everyone in Moscow seemed to snarl and tip their hat towards the wind as if to say, "Enough already."

I had continued at the rehab, riding the bus over in the morning like a commuter going to an office job. And though I attended therapy religiously, I had not achieved a major breakthrough. Six months into my sojourn I was still wheelchair bound, but I was committed and surrounded by people, Saroja and Tatiana mainly, who wouldn't let hope die.

By the spring, I was able to carry on rudimentary conversations with ease. As a result, things were heating up in my slightly tempestuous and highly flirtatious relationship with Saroja. He would still tease me and roll his eyes whenever I wore a bright new shirt that my mom or sister had sent over from the U.S. "Americans," he would say, as if the addition of teal to the serious gray tones of the facility was just the most ridiculous thing he had ever seen. But then there would be a poke or a pinch someplace on my body and a smile, and the whole process of jest and tease became something of a routine that I looked forward to each morning.

Tatiana was a classic maternal Russian matchmaker, grabbing Saroja when we would go off on our breaks and whispering the word "cake" or "tea" as she passed, like someone dealing in contraband. Those were easy days. I shared in the optimism of the season. Parks that were once stark pen-and-ink drawings of snow and bark shimmered with the iridescent green of new foliage. Flowers never seemed as rich and varied to me. People were everywhere: walking with babies and strolling through verdant urban landscapes that allowed them to escape the crass reality of their lives, even if just for an afternoon. Though I was still very much an outsider, I had the feeling that the worst was over for them, for us. But as is often the case, things sometimes need to get worse before they get better.

One day, I wore a gray sweatshirt to the rehab. I was already there when Saroja arrived. He walked towards me with his usual cocky strut.

"Debrey Ootrah." Good morning, I told him, offering up a satisfactory though not overzealous smile.

"Good morning," he said, yawning. *"Gotova?"* You ready?

"Almost," I said. And with that I grabbed the bottom of my sweatshirt and lifted it over my head, revealing a white T-shirt with a large American flag waving on the front. Below the flag were the words, "God Bless the USA!" I brought it with me more as a personal memento of home, a comfort blanket that I never expected to wear in public. But I felt that my relationship with Saroja had matured to the point where it could handle high stakes taunting and I was right.

"Oh no!" He cried in Russian, laughing outright and covering his eyes as if he was faced with something so hideous that he couldn't bear to look. Then came more laughter on both our parts. I waited for my well earned poke and instead found that his ritualized jab had been replaced by a long, soft touch on my side and that his hand wasn't going away. He looked down at me smiling like someone who had finally given in to the inevitable. From that day forward Saroja and I began to spend time together outside of the rehab.

The next month or so was punctuated by excursions to Moscow's more bucolic settings. A day in the park was one of the few romantic devices available to the cash-strapped Russian male during the final days of the Soviet era. There were no fancy dinners or evenings at the theater with which to stack his deck. Saroja, ever the survivor, assessed his resources and we hop-scotched our way through Moscow's parks and gardens as therapist and patient became boyfriend and girlfriend.

Saroja was my first experience with the kind of emotional connection that allows two people to communicate through osmosis. We could say nothing when we were together yet understand everything. I suppose that I was initially attracted to him because he always gave me such a hard time and pretended that he didn't need anything that I could possibly offer him. He really couldn't care less that I was American, unlike most of the other guys that I met in Russia. For most, I was at best a representative of something fresh and optimistic, something that they had tasted through movies and books and that they wanted more of. At worst I was money, a possible way out of their grim setting or simply a way to avoid the breadline for a while. All the material things and even some of the more conceptual attributes, the elements of the American brand (freedom, openness, optimism), simply did not impress him. Saroja wanted more.

We can all learn from Saroja. He didn't just take things at face value. He wasn't panicking like his comrades, overwhelmed by uncertainty, and trying to jump ship like frightened passengers in the face of impending doom. Saroja was a man at a young age. And by that I mean he was able to take a step back, look at the situation at hand, and realize who he was, what was happening, and how he could best get through it with his pride and dignity intact. That is probably still what I appreciate most about him to this day.

Somehow, and I really have no idea how it happened, we ended up living together. We were such an odd pair. That I, a young woman from Louisiana, in a wheelchair, would end up living in an obscure Moscow apartment block with a Russian man was about as far off the Life game board as you could get. Nonetheless, it worked—we worked. I connected to his gumption and his ability to rise above the current situation. I connected to his pride and his strong sense of self. He found the same in me.

And thus, what had started half a year earlier as a search for a cure for paralysis slowly morphed into something else. Suddenly, I found myself drawn into the lives of the people there, Saroja specifically, but also many other sweet people who made me feel very much at home in a far away and alien land. I began to sense that while my legs were still not working, another wounded part of my identity was being rehabilitated in Russia. I was no longer overwhelmed and laid fallow by shame. I felt pretty. In the heady Moscow spring, I was once again woman.

Taking Control by Choosing to Savor the Good

My appreciation for the resiliency and survival instincts of the Russian people did not blind me to the harsh reality of their struggle. In fact, when Saroja and I moved in together, I got up close and personal with the situation "on the street" and was often stunned and saddened by the desperate nature of things. For him, the struggle facing the Russian people challenged their very identity and continued viability as a culture and society. Their self-sufficiency was of paramount importance to him. He had the perspective, not misguided I might add, that if they weren't able to care for themselves they would be lost. Sound familiar? It should, because my Russian friends were struggling against adversity very much in the same way I was. We each were being forced to face life without resources that we had once taken for granted. They could no longer rely on the state to take care of them from cradle to grave and would have to redefine themselves and find a new way to survive. And more than that, to live meaningful lives. In this way, their experience greatly paralleled my own.

As a result of his philosophy, Saroja refused to eat the bananas and peanut butter that I was able to buy at the *Beriozkas* or hard currency stores. I have to say that it made him even more attractive to me. He wouldn't accept any handouts or material assistance and chose instead to rely on the black market, disappearing for hours at a time and coming back home with meats and cheeses. It was kind of exciting, except that at the end of the night all of the intrigue and suspense might have been over a stick of bologna. Still, I knew not to ask too many questions because it was very serious and a matter of subsistence for many people. And thus meals became symbolic banters that let Saroja feel he was honoring his fellow Russians by suffering along with them. If I had a banana he munched on pickled herring. If I made a peanut butter sandwich, he sliced himself a piece of contraband cheese. But I am sure that our well-stocked cupboards provided a level of comfort for him.

Our flat was in a classic Russian apartment block near Gorky Park. There were the drab hallways common to most large apartment buildings constructed in the 1950s, and as you passed each door you could smell all sorts of things cooking on old gas stoves that people lit with thick wooden matches. Chicken cutlets frying in pans and hearty stews—all of it seeped under the front doors and taunted the senses of passersby. The hallway was a virtual olfactory catalogue of the food being sold clandestinely on the black market in dank alleys and dark vestibules all over Moscow.

With my Russian lover came Russian in-laws, so to speak. Luckily for me, Saroja came from a wonderful family. I was always welcomed in their home and was usually the center of attention at any family gathering, which typically involved not only his immediate family but cousins and aunts and uncles. There were adults arguing politics, making toasts to this uncle or that aunt for a witty insight, and laughing children who filled the house with optimism. Each gathering was a true celebration of life. These people, and the many other families just like them, embodied the power of positive thinking and the wisdom of taking stock in what you have rather than what you lack. For them, at that time, their greatest asset was each other and together they felt confident that they would make it through intact to whatever outcome was in store for their beloved homeland.

And while Saroja's family embraced me with open arms, his uncle, Valoidia, who was a sturgeon fisherman, took a special liking to me. He was a rather shadowy and swarthy figure and Saroja looked up to him. If the world was crumbling, you wouldn't know it by looking at Valoidia. He was doing just fine. "I am from the Black Sea; very beautiful. Saroja, you must bring her," he said. I had visions of him sauntering down cobblestone streets in some sultry seaside town, filled with handsome, tanned men pitched in café doorways, eyes flicking from side to side. I based this fantasy on my impression of Valoidia, who seemed both rough and suave at the same time. I told him how much I liked caviar and the next time he came to visit, he brought me a whole mason jar full of beluga. There might not have been bread in the shops, but Saroja and I used to kick back on our couch and eat caviar out of the jar with a spoon.

Saroja and his family also introduced me to the wonderful Russian tradition called the *Dacha*. The Dacha is a simple weekend home that people maintain outside of the city where they can escape the urban landscape and commune with nature. Most families grow fruits and vegetables on the small plot of land surrounding the house. It's kind of like dollhouses set in a communal garden filled with beautiful flowers and squash and string beans. Out in the Dacha, neighboring families often come together to eat and drink surrounded by the lush green foliage. The Dacha became a valuable respite for weary Muscovites.

I remember the first weekend a few of us went off to the Dacha. I cleaned my own strawberries and Saroja helped his father put up a new house. To the unassimilated American eye, the house in the Dacha was a tiny three room shack, but to us it was beautiful and the living that went on around it was as inspiring as the clean air perfumed by flowers and earth.

Meanwhile, back in Moscow, our flat became a gathering place for all of Saroja's friends, who quickly became my friends too. While the weekdays were still about rehab, where we continued to play our respective roles of patient and therapist, the weekends had become a time of celebration. Every Saturday night, friends would come, each with a dish to contribute so that our table was full of tasty Russian delights like dumplings, potatoes, and cabbage and all sorts of simple but delicious dishes. Everywhere I went, people seemed to be coming together.

And so it was that in the midst of a geopolitical mess wrought with hardships and uncertainty I found a kind of honest happiness that came from people who felt like they were on the verge extinction. I connected to my Russian friends on levels that both astonished and inspired me. We had all experienced a horrific loss. Our identities were being challenged and we all felt as if we had lost our grip on destiny. In a way, we had both gone from superpower to survivor in a short period of time. It was this level of identification that allowed me to achieve an intimacy with Saroja that was impossible with Tom back in Boulder.

The Passing of an Era

Over a year had passed since my first night at the Hotel Zvezdnaya. My relationship with Saroja had strengthened. Tatiana and I still worked together, though not every day. Dikool still barked orders at the staff. And I still could not walk. The only thing that had changed was the political situation. It was clear that things couldn't continue to teeter on the way they had for the past several years. All around, countries which were under the influence of Russia since WWII, enclosed behind the so called Iron Curtain, had begun to rebel and break from Moscow. This had a dramatic impact on the Russian psyche. For the past two or three years, the people in the Soviet Union felt like they were in a building falling down in slow motion. But that was about to change. The final stages of collapse would be lighting fast.

In August of 1990, Saroja and I were returning from a weekend in the Dacha with our friend Dima. As we approached Moscow, the roads were torn to shreds. Closer to the center of town we found ourselves in the midst of a massive traffic jam. We were at a standstill for so long that Dima jumped out of the car and started talking to nearby cabbies, asking them, *"Shot takoi?"* What's going on? *"Perevarod,"* they shouted back. I didn't understand and pleaded with them to explain.

"Carlana, eta revolutsii!" Dima yelled emphatically. Revolution. A group of hardliners was trying to stave off inevitable change as the state approached its final death throes. They tried to hold back the rising tide of discontent, which was preparing to sweep them out of power and into the history books.

I thought, *Oh my God! I'm in the middle of a Russian revolution!*

A mixture of fear and excitement pulsed through me. On the one hand, it was exciting because it seemed that the winds of democracy which had been blowing in from the West were finally beginning to affect change. On the other hand, it seemed that there were people in charge who were prepared to go down with the ship and, I worried, perhaps take everyone with them.

After sitting in traffic for about six hours, we managed to make it past the American embassy. Cars were overturned and soldiers were poised behind them with machine guns at the ready. It was a tense and scary scene but Saroja and Dima didn't flinch. We made it to our friend Andrei's house where we spent the next few days. When I phoned the American embassy for information and advice I was told that they didn't even have me on record as being in the country. It was important that I be registered, I was told, in case they issued a state of emergency and a war broke out. Otherwise I would be on my own. It took two days before I was able to get a line out to my parents. My father contacted our senator in Washington who telexed the embassy about my case. I was finally registered by phone.

I asked the staff at the American embassy what I should be doing and they told me to watch CNN. I remember thinking, *Sure, I live in a Russian apartment with Russian people. Great advice.* My TV had maybe three stations, all of which had stopped broadcasting. Thank God I had Saroja. He made me feel more secure than my fellow countrymen during those tense days.

Papers and everything else considered left-wing were also closed and we only heard the pathetic socialist dribble that seeped out of the Kremlin. The attempt at total control shocked my American sensibilities. Thankfully though, at that point in history, there was no turning back. The Russian people simply wouldn't have it.

We eventually learned that coup leaders had declared Gorbachev too ill to govern. Gorbachev meanwhile was under house arrest in the Crimea, a resort area on the Black Sea. The people took to the streets and I was able to watch and feel the wave of change finally crest over Moscow. In an attempt to subdue the population, the coup leaders called in the army. Instead of suppressing the masses, the soldiers sided with the demonstrators and the coup collapsed. It was for me perhaps the most profound example of people taking charge of their destiny.

A few days later Gorbachev was reinstated. The Russian people, in their unwillingness to sit back and be victims of the failed ideology of a few old men, had finally been heard. By December all of the soviet republics had declared their independence from Moscow. An era for the Russia people had passed. And in many ways, it had for me too.

Perestroika

Perestroika was the program of reform that led to the end to the Soviet socialist system. The word literally means restructuring or reordering and is therefore both an end and a beginning. From Moscow to the Czech Republic, people demanded a change to the way their countries, and thus their lives, were run. They knew that an era had passed and they demanded a new perspective.

The majority of people in Russia understood that the old system could no longer sustain them. They knew that it was time to let go of the past and move on to a different and hopefully better future. But there were some who were frightened about what change might bring, especially the old timers. They worried that they might be lost in the new world order. They worried about what the loss of the socialist safety net would mean for them. Would they have food and shelter provided to them as it had been before? Also, though they usually articulated fears about practical things, I am sure that they must have worried a bit about their own identity as a people, about what being Russian would mean after the changeover.

Saroja and all my Russian friends were optimistic and focused on the future and what their roles would be in their, governmentally speaking, new nation. Clearly there was a great deal of uncertainty that came with their new situation. They too worried about mundane things that had once been guaranteed as a birthright—things like jobs and housing. But for Saroja and his friends, with uncertainty came a sense of potential. These were people who were armed with a perspective of optimism in the face of adversity. The strong souls who were able to see their cup half-full despite their often hopeless circumstances. Besides helping them to survive great hardships, it allowed them to see opportunities. And they made sure that, when the time came, they would be ready to seize them.

As for me, I arrived in Russia a frustrated and restless soul and over my two years there became a person much more aware of her blessings. I had learned another language, witnessed history in the making, and experienced my first serious relationship. They didn't "fix" me; I couldn't walk and the therapy hadn't worked as I had hoped. However, after two years in Russia, my definition of cure had changed and I realized that I was the only one who had the power to heal my deepest wounds, those that went beyond the physical to become scars on the soul. I was finally getting close to the sentiment embodied by Anatoly's "rising."

As much as I cared for and loved Saroja and all of my friends in Moscow, it was clear to me that my future did not lie with them. I was ready to move on and take on the next great adventure. They were ready to start their own journey, to build a future in the new Russia. My time in Moscow helped open my eyes the amazing opportunities that were available to me. The change in my world-view was comprehensive in nature.

In Boulder I came off as someone at peace with herself and in total control. I did everything possible to hide the pain and insecurity caused by my paralysis from the world around me. After my time in Moscow, I had become much more like the strong and centered person that I had claimed to be all along. My experience and the new outlook that it afforded me enabled me to take back some of the power that I had relinquished to my chair.

As a result, I felt a renewed sense of hope and was ready to return home, finish school, and build my future.

Lesson Learned: *I Smell a Rut*

I could have stayed in Russia and perhaps married. I might have been a translator or a tour guide and spent weekends in the country with my animated Russian family. And I am sure that I would have been loved and embraced. Instinct, however, told me that the life Russia had to offer wasn't the right one for me.

At first I didn't want to accept what my instinct was telling me because it meant change and leaving people that I cared for. But while I didn't like the idea of change, I hated the idea of stagnation and regret. I had not finished college and this was a constant source of angst for me. More than that, I was finally thinking in terms of *doing* rather than *fixing* and the shift in focus brought a great sense of excitement to my life, one that I was eager to explore. My time in Russia had begun with a quest for "the cure" and after two years I was ready to embrace "the now."

When I decided to leave Russia and return to the U.S., I chose personal growth over comfort. It was confusing, because staying in Russia felt like the safe thing to do. But I listened to my gut, my inner compass, did a lot of soul searching and was able to build a case to support my decision. I felt as if I had reached a proverbial fork in the road and my instinct helped me decide which direction to take. This is when I realized I had found another important rule to live by:

KNOW WHEN TO LET GO

It is easy to stay in one place even when we know it's not healthy or fulfilling. It means staying with the familiar, with what we know. But in the long-term we definitely suffer. I know so many people who have stuck with dead-end jobs or unfulfilling relationships only to become depressed and overwhelmed with feelings of regret. They become deadened to the world and mourn their squandered potential. I have also seen frustration turn to anger and watched friends lash out at the people around them. I am happy that I decided to leave Russia before the magic was gone.

I feel like life is a series of stages and that we are all on growth tangents that take us through various emotional and, as in my case, geographic landscapes. Sometimes the breaks between the stages are easy to see. We know that we have grown and that it is time to move on. For example, young people graduating from college know that their world is about to change radically. It is clear that they are moving from a period of dependency to one of self-sufficiency (at least their parents hope so).

As we get older the lines between life stages become more subtle and blurry, and sometimes in turn we become unable or unwilling to acknowledge them. This can cause us to lose our positive momentum and get, in all senses of the word, stuck. Like the Russians afraid of life in the new world order, when it's up to us, we often can't seem to let go of situations that run their course and offer little hope for long-term happiness. But by being honest with ourselves and heeding our gut, we won't confuse stagnation for comfort and as a result will suffer fewer regrets.

I've known Carrie for most of my life. Ever since we were little girls, she dreamed of falling in love, having the big wedding, and moving into a house with a white picket fence. You know, the quintessential American Dream. Well, at thirty-eight, Carrie was not married and had been dating a man for nearly four years. They moved in together a year after they met and from the outside looking in, things seemed perfect. He was a caring man and let her know that he considered her his friend and partner. He even proclaimed his love for her. She, in turn, cared for him and valued their relationship. They were exclusive.

So far, so good. The relationship seemed grounded. There was no hostility or ill-will. They loved the same food, liked the same movies, and shared an intimate group of friends. They were by those means perfect for one another. The problem was, deep down, they had very different basic needs. Needs that weren't going away.

After living together for nearly three years, Carrie finally told Tim that she wanted to get married and that she wanted to have children. She was very aware of her biological clock ticking.

Tim, however, who is older that Carrie, already had two children from a previous marriage. From the beginning he told her that he had no desire to marry again or have any more children. His first marriage ended so badly that he went for many years without even seeing his son and daughter.

Real commitment, in the way the Carrie wanted, seemed out of the question. Rather than addressing the issues head-on and accepting his stance, she lived each day insisting that she could change him. She believed that he'd come around and be the man she wanted him to be. She believed that he would be able to meet her needs.

"Am I that naïve to believe we have something?" she asked me once.

We sat down and made a list of the things in her life that were causing her the greatest anxiety. Number one on her list was her relationship with Tim. Next came her job, which she had been neglecting because she was so distracted by her relationship issues. Finances came in a distant third.

The latter two issues were manageable. But we discussed the fact that she and Tim had two completely different expectations from their relationship. Tim's needs were being met by the nature of the relationship. But Carrie's needs were revealing themselves to be more central in her life than she realized. Moreover, since they were unmet, she felt unfulfilled.

I left her with the three issues written down on a piece of paper. She kept the paper out and even showed it to Tim. The act of seeing, in black and white, the correlation between her relationship and lack of fulfillment was a catalyst for her. Over time, Carrie began to accept that Tim was not capable of giving her what she wanted.

They decided to try a trial break-up. But not long after, Tim moved back in. They both didn't know how to cope with the idea of being alone. Carrie swore that he was different. She said that he was very affectionate and more caring than before. He seemed more sensitive to her needs. However, in the end, Tim still insisted that he didn't want to get married or have children. So really, the separation accomplished nothing. It was the familiarity that kept them together and the fear of the unknown that kept them from trying to begin anew.

So there was Carrie, almost a year later, her relationship like an unlucky hand of Monopoly: she was stuck owning the railroads when she had her heart set on Park Place or Boardwalk. Still she couldn't let go. She cried on my shoulder, telling me how much she loved him and believed in a future with Tim.

When people become involved, they need to understand and accept the expectations and goals of their mate. People need to protect their hearts. Carrie allowed a dead-end relationship to go on too long, even though her partner was honest about his intentions. Her refusal to accept his position consumed precious time that might have been filled with a flourishing relationship that met her needs.

Carrie just recently let go of the notion that she and Tim would be together forever. She is focusing on and enjoying her successful career in real estate and spending time with old friends. Everyone has been supportive. Letting go hurt, but Carrie has a new-found hope and her self-esteem is rising. The nice thing is that she and Tim remain close friends. However, she is now looking for someone who will be able to meet her basic needs and accepts that she will never be fulfilled with Tim. Carrie is living proof that knowing when to let go can liberate you and help you avoid unnecessary distractions on your own precious path to happiness and fulfillment.

If you feel like you are in a rut and not living up to your potential because you should have moved on from your current situation long ago, it is never too late to take action. When pulling yourself out of a rut means making a significant, overdue life change, it can be accomplished through careful planning and with fewer negative social implications than in years past. Here are some exercises that may be useful.

· EXERCISES ·

The bridge

When we are born, we are attached to our mothers by an umbilical cord. The first thing a doctor does is separate the two lives. The child grows to become an adult. Later in life, the emotional cord is cut and the child is off on his or her way to independence. Sometimes we find ourselves in relationships where the cord needs to be broken. The connection is no longer a healthy one and it is simply time to move on.

When you find yourself trapped in a dead-end relationship, try to visualize a healthy exit. Visualize that you and your partner are on a bridge and attached by a rope. You know that to release yourself of the continued feelings of sadness and frustration, you must fully cut the rope so that you are no longer attached. An intact rope keeps you continuously feeding on each other's emotions and anxiety. If one falls, the other goes with them.

Imagine yourself severing the rope and moving on with your life. Keep visualizing the process. Know that just like a baby with a freshly cut umbilical cord, you will heal over time. Eventually, after repeatedly visualizing severing the rope, you will find that it is easier to actually carry out the separation, which is best for both parties in the long term.

· · · ·

Traffic light

Think of the stressful situations you have been in or are in right now. List them. Examples: being in a dead-end relationship; applying for a job; talking to family members about a conflict; being alone, and so on.

Now, align your warning signals for stress. By each stress, put the color RED, YELLOW, or GREEN. Of course RED means immediate attention, YELLOW is a warning, and GREEN means that you have it under control.

Use the results of this test to figure out what needs immediate attention and also those things that can wait.

Once you determine which issues need immediate attention, write down three things that you can do to address them. Write down one immediate step, one near-term step, and one long-term step that will ultimately resolve the matters completely.

CHAPTER 8

An Unexpected Setback

• •

The Power of Positive Thinking

The skies over Moscow were battleship gray the day I left for the U.S. It was a common shade but nonetheless a fitting and sullen backdrop for the emotions surging through me. *How could I leave?* I thought. I felt like my heart was being ripped to pieces because I knew that the next time I saw Saroja things would be very different. Torn between duty and desire, I said goodbye to a period, a place, and a lover. And it hurt.

When I boarded the jet there was some confusion over seat assignments. One thing led to another and I found myself upgraded and sitting in first class. I strained to look out the window at what I knew would be my last glimpse of Russia for a long time. As we raced down the runway for takeoff, the different greens and tans of the airfield became a blur, and just like the last flickering frames of a home movie Russia slipped away.

I remember that they had all sorts of delicacies on the plane. Anyone lucky enough to have flown Pan Am first class knows what I am talking about. They really knew how to pamper their passengers.

You would think that after spending so much time living on peanut butter and whatever Russian food Saroja and our friends could scrape together, I would have been overjoyed to indulge in champagne and steak. Instead, they offered a hollow pleasure. Perhaps I was sad and distracted. But I think that my time in Russia had taught me about the inherent value of things. I recalled with great fondness our many potluck suppers and the warmth that the humble dishes represented. As Dickens wrote, "It was the best of times. It was the worst of times."

Shreveport had become a stranger to me. It was still home, where I was raised, but it no longer had the same sense of intimacy that it once did. I had fallen out of rhythm with the place. I enjoyed being there but was aware that it was merely a layover on the way to the next stage of my life. As I acclimated myself to life in the U.S., I took time to drive down the lanes and country routes around town. Places that were once the center of my universe were now haunted with old memories. It was settling, though, to go home and be surrounded by the unconditional love of people who had known me all my life.

My first goal was college. I was now many years behind the people I started school with in Boulder and felt pressure to try and catch up with them. But I was also excited to go back to school because I now had a focus. My immersion in Russian language and culture coupled with the dramatic time period of my sojourn was an invaluable educational experience; one I wanted to parlay into a degree in Slavic studies. Most schools would have loved to have a unique student like me, a witness to recent history. But back in Boulder I had been more concerned with people liking me and not writing me off as a cripple than studying. As a result, my grades were poor and my GPA very low. It was going to be a challenge to find a school that would trust me to perform.

Not long after I returned home, I paid a visit to San Francisco and a friend at the University of California at Berkeley. All it took was an afternoon on the campus and I was hooked. I knew I had found my next home. The challenge was going to be getting in. Why would Berkeley, a so-called "public ivy," accept a student like me? On paper, academically speaking, I was a disaster.

I decided to put Tatiana's strategy to work and see my cup as half full. I felt that despite my performance in Boulder, my unique experience and the dramatic events that had just unfolded in Russia presented an opportunity. Hopeful, I stopped by the Slavic studies department where I met briefly with the department head and told him my story. His eyes twinkled as I explained in perfect Russian how an experimental surgery led to two years in Moscow and a ringside seat to, what was at that time, the recent collapse of the Soviet Union. I explained my past and implored him to help me get into the university and earn a spot in his department.

I was persistent and passionate. I even wrote an essay that acknowledged the errors of my past academic ways but drove home the richness of my experience and my desire and commitment to get as much out of it as possible. I positioned myself as a student able to bring invaluable insight on contemporary

Russian culture and events into the classroom. My determination paid off and the opportunity opened up. I was admitted into Berkeley in the fall of 1992. I graduated with honors in 1995. Tatiana would have been proud.

Live from Miami Beach

Graduating from a prestigious university with honors was an important benchmark for me and marked the beginning of what I hoped would be a period of professional achievement and growth. Fixing my damaged spinal cord and learning to walk again were no longer my life's sole focus. I hadn't given up completely, but I would channel my energies into goals that I could achieve under my own power. Russia drove home the fact that life is not a dress rehearsal. I didn't want to wait for a breakthrough or chase after long-shots before I began living. In that way, succeeding at Berkeley was more than a degree; it was a passport to realizing my potential.

But what to do with an aberrant degree like a BA in Slavic studies? Most people in the department went on to graduate studies or to a job at one of the non-profit organizations or governmental agencies doing work in Russia. I considered both options briefly, but a chance conversation would open the door to the next phase of my life and take me to yet another distinctive city.

My family was quite active in a fantastic organization called the Miami Project to Cure Paralysis. The organization, based in Miami, Florida, is a one of the world's leading research centers for spinal cord injuries. Through our involvement, we met the doctor and philanthropist that started the organization and kept in touch with him over the years. After I graduated from Berkeley, I called him and told him that I was looking for something to do with my life. He was a well-connected man and I thought he, if anyone, might have had some leads for me.

He informed me that he had recently started Project Medishare, a small organization which was dedicated to improving the healthcare infrastructure in Haiti. It was also based in Miami and enjoyed close ties to the city's medical community. He said that they were looking for someone with gusto and drive to help build some momentum and interest in the project, and, having known me many years, thought that I would make a great executive director. Opportunity number two had just come my way.

Within three weeks I packed up my life in San Francisco and drove cross-country to Miami. There is something empowering about embarking on a long road-trip to start a new life. I highly recommend the experience. You find yourself lost in contemplation and, if you're driving through the West, feeding off of the energy of the landscape. It was awesome.

A while back I had received word that Karen Jordan, the woman with whom I shared a room in rehab just after the accident, had passed away. Like many quadriplegics, she didn't live very long. Her story pains me because it defies reason. But that's part of life. Sometimes the explanation eludes us and we can only hope that some day we will be able to connect the dots. Anyway, I knew in my heart that she was in a better place and when I drove through Texas, I said a prayer and spoke to her for a few moments. Maybe it was a phenomenon caused by the emptiness of the landscape, a canvas on which the mind has ample room to play, but I had the feeling that Karen was right there by my side.

The Supermodels and Me

If Moscow was a colorless monument to the oppressive Soviet regime, Miami was a flashy tropical songbird. I was struck by the youthful energy of the city and the sun-drenched colors of the Art Deco buildings. Miami was light years away from Moscow and the antithesis of the intellectual and cultured Bay Area. It seemed like people would have to struggle to be unhappy there. Miami was, quite simply, hot.

Everyone knows that the city is a haven for beautiful people. I pulled into town just when South Beach was becoming chic. Until then I had been living in cold places and for the first time since the accident found myself in a city where bathing suits were considered casual dress. I had come a long way, but I was still loath to show my legs in public, especially when it seemed like there were supermodels flaunting their flesh on every street corner.

Like most carpetbaggers, I lived out of a hotel room before settling in the perfect condo on Brickell Key, a swanky neighborhood of high-rise residential towers on an island adjacent to downtown Miami. At the time, Brickell Key had a reputation for being the preferred domicile of the hip crowd in Miami. After years of daunting rehab, Russian political angst, and crunchy California intellectuals, I was ready for a little hedonism. I felt as though I had earned my right to rub shoulders with all the tan lovelies that seemed untouched by tragedy and pain. My address was going to act as a launch pad into the A-list nightlife circuit.

As a result of its tropical latitude, pools are the salons of Miami. "Let's go to the pool. I wonder who's down at the pool." A lot happens at the pool. It was a little like living at Club Med, which is exactly the kind of hedonistic atmosphere I was hoping to find. I even braved exposing my legs at the pool after I got the requisite tan on my balcony. And after just one week of pool time, I felt like I knew each tenant by name. Everything was on target with my expectations.

While I met lots of people, one of the first friends I made in Miami was a hot tamale from Puerto Rico named Brenda. She was dating a guy in my condo complex who liked me to give all his new girlfriends the once over as a form of "psycho" insurance. He and Brenda didn't last very long. Nearly twelve years later, Brenda is still one of my best friends.

I think we bonded because we recognized the survivor in each other. Brenda was and still is a pretty girl with a peppery attitude. Together we had our share of fun, but she was first and foremost a mother to her two little girls. It was at times a very hard life. The father of her children was a complete deadbeat and she faithfully managed to care for her daughters all by herself. We were still in our twenties and while other women her age were out on the town and partying till dawn, Brenda was often at home trying to figure out a way to stretch her money so that her children would never have to go without. She provided them with structure and ensured that those two little girls could be proud of themselves and their mother.

She could have stayed in Puerto Rico and lived a comfortable if uninspired life, but left because she wanted something better for herself and her kids. I chose challenge over comfort on several occasions. We had a lot in common. We were both women who had fought for a place in the sun.

She, like all of us, had her weak moments and would come to me when her problems seemed too much to bear. Other people, strangers even, feel comfortable telling me their problems. It's a phenomenon that makes going to the supermarket an interesting experience. And while it always feels good to be there for someone when they are hurting, I felt proud to offer Brenda some sense of consolation. I had myself to care for, but she had two little lives in her hands and she never lost sight of that. It's not surprising that in the end it would be Brenda who would give me the dose of tough love that would finally wrest me free from my demons.

Overconfidence Breeds Danger

When I accepted the job as the executive director of Project Medishare, I was loosely aware of the tragic situation in Haiti. My focus was Eastern Europe, not the Caribbean. But once I understood the scope of the suffering in Haiti, I was quickly swept up in the mission of the organization and took their plight to heart. The country was in shambles and almost devoid of any social services. Russia, with its crumbling hospitals, was absolutely first-rate compared to Haiti.

As the executive director, I traveled back and forth to the country with groups of doctors from the UN and Miami bigwigs. Often my work reminded me of what I learned in Russia: we Americans take so much for granted. Here was a Third World country right in America's backyard and it was a pitiful sight. The fifty-minute flight between Miami and Port-au-Prince was tantamount to time travel. The people had almost nothing. They were traumatized on many levels, often suffering illness and blighted by a lack of hope.

I finally understood why they thought I would be a good person to lead the organization. After what I had been through in terms of my physical and emotional distress, I was able to identify with these people in a fundamental way. I wanted to do what I could to help ease them out of their suffering. More than that, I found comfort in helping them—in making their lives better.

I am proud to say that our little organization managed to bring generators and all kinds of desperately needed medical equipment to hospitals in Haiti. It wasn't easy talking companies into donating extremely valuable equipment to a country that most considered a total basket case. But then there would be that one person who would listen to my plea and recall that they had something in stock, perhaps on older model incubator or some other life-giving device, which they would be able to secure as a donation for us.

When I wasn't talking people into donating equipment and expertise, I was raising money for the organization. I would invite Miami's business and cultural elites to fundraisers in support of Project Medishare. I loved this part of my job. My dad is a natural MC and I take after him. People were drawn to the air of southern hospitality that I projected and intrigued by the unique portrait I painted. I simply wasn't what most people expected a girl in a wheelchair to be like. I was always flirty, glammed up, and looking hot. I also wasn't just another pretty debutante standing up for a charity. The chair gave me the credibility to serve as an ambassador for people facing adversity.

The payback was huge. Whatever resources I managed to get over to the people in Haiti came back to me threefold in the form of self-satisfaction. Being able to go out into the field and see my hard work and good intentions translate into tangible benefits strengthened my spirit and gave my professional life profound meaning.

It also made me feel powerful. Here I was helping other people improve their lives. Me, the girl who nearly eight years earlier worried about being sidelined. I had overcome so much, fought so hard to make it back to the world, that I felt invulnerable. I believed that my personal and professional victories reflected an unshakable capacity to handle anyone or any situation I found myself in. If I hadn't been broken yet, I reasoned, what could possibly threaten me? It was a provocative assertion that, like the false sense of security I felt in James's arms on the night of the accident, blinded me to danger and would lead me down dark paths once more.

One evening I attended a fundraiser for the Miami Project. I was just a guest and I remember that I did my best to look like a starlet that night. The event was a gala affair, with many of Miami's wealthiest families represented. Everyone in the room was either very successful or from a wealthy family or both. In other words, it was the perfect place to meet a man. During the dinner, a handsome guy at another table caught my eye and it wasn't long before he walked across the room and introduced himself.

"Hi, I'm Jeff," he said, holding out his hand for me to shake. He was nearly six feet tall, had reddish brown hair, and the wholesome good looks of an Irish prize fighter. And though he was dressed up I could tell that he worked out or played sports.

"I'm Carlana," I responded, taking his hand and offering him a seat.

"Carlana, now that's a name. Nice to meet you, Carlana," he said, mimicking my southern accent.

What a night. I learned that he was the son of an old Miami family with ties to politics. He ran his own company and lived in a town not far from Miami. We talked and talked and I experienced that timeless sensation that occurs when you really connect with someone and the world seems to fall away.

At the end of the evening he escorted me to my car and kissed me goodnight. He was the first guy since Saroja that sent shivers down my spine. We made a date for the weekend, and I can honestly say that I literally went to sleep with a smile on my face that night.

Over the next several weeks, Jeff and I saw a lot of each other. He knew everyone and it felt great being on the arm of a good-looking guy at the hottest restaurants and bars in town. The more time we spent together the better looking he became. Moreover, I liked being seen with him. I hate to admit it, but I felt validated. His presence overpowered the wheelchair. I felt like everyone who met me when I was with Jeff saw me as just a pretty woman out with her boyfriend. Our public outings fed my weakness to look to the outside for self-confidence. My old demon, insecurity about my physical defects and desirability as a woman, was very much still with me.

My memories of that period are an odd tango of Haitian strife and extended pillow talk over the phone. I was giddy all the time and joked that someone must have slipped me a Haitian love potion. I gleefully told my parents and sisters about him. I recited every delicious sentence that he served me to Brenda or anyone who would listen as if they were uttered by a bard that rivaled Shakespeare himself. I was so much in awe of him, so infatuated, that I didn't see the danger signs. Either inside of myself or in him.

Running with Blinders

Three months. Much can happen in that short span of time. Lives can change with subtlety each day so that three months' time can be as fundamentally transformational as the passing of one season into another. In my case, three months after our first date I found myself deeply in love with Jeff. Yet to which season I had arrived, whether it was one marked by death or rebirth, was not yet evident.

It's amazing that I was able to get any work done considering how distracted I was during the beginning of our relationship. Somehow I stayed focused enough at the office to continue raising money and securing donations for Project Medishare. Enough even to catch the eye of a man who would transform my life after seeing a flicker of my potential as a communicator.

At one of my fundraisers, I ran a slideshow that highlighted the decrepit nature of the hospitals in Haiti. I got up in front of the audience and narrated the piece, a tragic tale about babies who had perished because their hospitals lost power and had no back up generators to power their incubators—a sad and unfortunately true story designed to unlock checkbooks.

After my speech, I was approached by a man who introduced himself as the head of programming for Channel 10, the local ABC affiliate in Miami. "You are a talented young lady; the way you spoke was very powerful. You have a wonderful cause here," he said.

I thanked him and then he asked me if I ever thought about being on TV. I just laughed and said, "Yeah, right."

"I'm serious," he said and he gave me his card and told me to contact him at the station. As he walked away, I looked at the card in my hand and muttered to myself, "...yeah, right."

The next night Jeff came over. I opened the door and he threw his arms around me and scooped me right out of my wheelchair. We necked in the doorway of the condo like newlyweds crossing the threshold.

The magic didn't last long. "Nadine!" he bellowed, in a convincing redneck cadence. He used to poke fun at my southern accent by imitating Brad Pitt in the movie *Kalifornia*. Yet another warning if you've ever seen the movie.

After he came in and got settled I showed him the business card from the station director and told him what had happened the night before. He stood examining the card in his hands, tilting it back and forth as if there was a glare on it. I think I was holding a glass of wine at the time. I remember glancing up at him and seeing a look of concentration on his face, his nose all crinkled, like he was trying to make sense of the words on the card.

"Can't believe they'd put a gimp on TV," he said, tossing the card onto the counter.

My heart skipped a beat. His words crackled through me like and electric shock. In an instant I was back on the board trying to shimmy my way out of my parents' car as a bunch of onlookers gawked in horror and pity at my useless legs. In an instant my hard work and progress was called into question. I tried to process the words. *Gimp*. The word stung like a dentist poking a bad nerve. Looking up at him from my chair, from what suddenly seemed like a great distance, all I could bring myself to say was, "What?"

He just watched me, gauging my reaction. After a few seconds his face relaxed and opened up, his grimace morphing into a smile.

"Just kidding," he said, pinching my cheek affectionately. "So you gonna call him?" he asked.

"No, I don't think so," I responded, taking a hefty sip of my drink and changing the subject as quickly as possible. The rest of the evening was uneventful. I tried to forget about the incident, but all night long the word gimp kept invading my thoughts like a giant blinking neon sign. I recall a few forced laughs on my part before we made love and I was left to ponder the word in the dark as Jeff snored softly beside me.

I eventually rationalized the incident and chalked the whole thing up to his cocky sense of humor. I watched his chest rise and fall, and as I admired his beautiful, seemingly unflawed body, I was annoyed with myself for being so sensitive. I snuggled up close to him and drifted off to sleep.

Slipping into Darkness

It is funny how patterns can emerge. You meet someone or move to a new place and little by little you find yourself frequenting the same coffee shop in the morning, taking the same route to work everyday, or thinking about things vis-à-vis someone else in a certain fashion.

This is what had begun that evening. A pattern. I didn't know it then, but the sentence, his poisonous words, were the first volley in the ultimate battle for my salvation. A new friend can inspire a new perspective and an abuser can prey on vulnerabilities that confuse you into thinking you are somehow worthy of your treatment.

Until that evening, just being with Jeff built up my sense of desirability. To me, his presence told the world that I was worthy of love. I wore his affection like a merit badge. This is what made his attacks so painful.

I remember telling Brenda what had happened. I mentioned it casually while lying outside in the sun as her kids splashed around in my pool. She knew about the offer from the TV station and was curious about what my next steps were going to be.

"I don't know. I think it's all a little crazy. But I've been watching the news and I could see myself on there, you know?"

"You can totally do it. It's perfect. They'll love you. You kidding me?"

"Well, Jeff doesn't seem to think so."

She turned her head towards me, concerned and curious as to what I meant. "What d'ya mean?" She said.

"Oh, he made a stupid comment. A joke really."

"What'd he say?"

"It's stupid. But I wonder if others would think it."

"What?"

"He was teasing me and said that he couldn't believe they'd put a gimp on TV"

"What?" she shouted, turning to face me and planting her feet firmly on the concrete below her, "He said that to you? Are you serious?"

"He was just being a cocky son of a bitch, Bren. I told you how he is. Seriously, he was just kidding. It's no big deal. What's more important is he made me think that other people might think that way."

"Carlana, no one thinks that. What's important is that he doesn't think that way."

"Of course he doesn't. Why would he be with me?"

To this she had no response. At face value, it sounds like a waterproof defense. Why would someone who would say something so mean want to be with me, regardless if they meant it or not? The answer would not surface for some time yet. I would eventually discover that there were many reasons; long, twisted, convoluted reasons that implicated me as well him.

She turned around and lay back on the lounge chair. After a moment of silence she said, "Just make sure he doesn't say it again."

"He won't. It was just a stupid guy thing."

"No, it's just stupid. What a jerk," she said. Brenda does not mince words.

I decided then and there that I wouldn't talk about it anymore and definitely wouldn't share any future transgressions with Brenda. It was the first time that I made a conscious decision to conceal Jeff's behavior. I hadn't counted, however, on the swiftness of my slide into abuse and enablement. And how it would send me running to her for help.

A Toxic Combination

Over the next several months our relationship thickened like a toxic stew brewing on a hot stove. The more we simmered, the more our intrinsic flaws seeped out of us, the more we assumed our roles of abuser and victim. If we were ingredients in a chemist's lab our warning labels would have said, "Dangerous when mixed!"

During this thickening, as Jeff and I became entwined, fused, I drifted farther and farther away from the people I loved. Friends that I had known since Boulder and even earlier heard less and less from me. Brenda became one of the few people I continued to see. I was slowly beginning the long submerge.

It wasn't all bad. At least in the beginning. There were long stretches of normalcy interrupted by crescendos of hostility. All it took was the right trigger, a word, statement, or situation that he either disagreed with or found threatening and he would explode. Handsome hunk would become monster in a moment's notice. He was a real life Dr. Jekyll and Mr. Hyde. He gave me love and support only to pull the rug out from under me when I least expected it. It made the fall that much more painful.

Sometimes I would flat-out misread character flaws as something positive. An example of this was how I perceived his controlling nature. Once we were a dating, he wanted to be involved in all aspects of my life. In hindsight, this was one of his worst traits. He wanted to know where I was and who I was with twenty-four seven. He didn't even like me to go out with friends if he couldn't join us. If I went out for dinner with Brenda, I would come home to a series of messages escalating in tone from inquisitive, "It's me, call me back," to impatient, "It's nine o'clock, where are you?" to angry, "Where the hell are you? Call me the minute you get in." At least that's what I recall. It's all so distant now. In hindsight, it was insanity. But at the time I believed his wanting to control all aspects of my life was a sign of his affection for me. I thought that he wanted to protect me because he just couldn't bear the idea of me being out in the world alone and around other men that might find me attractive.

Jeff was more clever than I was in those early days. He understood my insecurities, the aspects of my identity that were directly tied to my disability. He knew that while I had an outgoing, positive attitude, deep down inside there were tender areas. We all have them, even if we are able to keep them hidden most of the time. But because my adversity was so public, it was easy to guess that mine were tied to my physical appearance and, ultimately, as a young vital woman, my desirability. He honed in on my insecurities like a shark to blood.

The odd thing is that I didn't resist him. I didn't tell him to go to hell like I should have. After an assault, I would cry and tell him I was sorry for whichever transgression I was accused. Looking back I'm stunned at my behavior. The more he taunted me the more I wanted to please him.

I thought that perhaps my experience with Saroja was a fluke. Saroja was a therapist after all, and was used to being with people like me. But not Jeff. Jeff was just a guy. Maybe he was right. Perhaps there weren't many people out there, let alone good looking, successful men like Jeff, who would want to be with me. My own sister once said that it was going to take a special kind of man to love me.

I became afflicted by a series of open-ended questions that drove me closer to disaster: *Maybe men really did think I was a freak? Maybe Jeff was the reality for people like me and the best that I could do?* I began to feel that I should be grateful for his affection.

He asked if he could move in. I said yes.

Lost in Enablement

As time moved forward there was less and less of the sweet romantic I fell in love with. He surfaced after a fight or on the occasions when I turned my back to him, when I showed my frustration with him and myself for not being able to change the situation. And when he was kind it was an all-encompassing love and warmth. This dichotomy made understanding the dynamics of our relationship very difficult. It also made it easy for me to rationalize. I had a way of making sense of the situation. For every bad trait, there was an explanation that made it tolerable. He's too jealous: So are many men, I reasoned. He's threatened by my attractiveness: Lot's of men can't handle strong independent women. He came from an abusive home and has got demons of his own: *He needs me,* I thought. I was quite the enabler.

I didn't share much with people because I thought that they wouldn't understand. Frankly, I thought that all I would do was disturb them with uncomfortable talk of domestic squabbles. I wasn't miserable yet. But I wasn't happy either. Every now and then I would tell Brenda something and she would get really pissed off. She begged me to dump him and move on. She kept telling me that I could do so much better. Funny, I couldn't even live up to my own insight. I was stuck. And at the time I thought it was simply the hard reality of my condition, not my relationship. It seemed that the season I had entered was a private winter—a period of despair and decay.

My private life would be thrust into the open one evening when Brenda and I came back to my building after a "girls' night out." We didn't go out often. She had two little girls and I had a live-in boyfriend. After walking me to my door, she intended to go upstairs to see my neighbor, whom she had been dating.

Before I could get my key in the door, Jeff opened it in a huff. He seemed furious with me. Brenda looked at me with an expression that revealed a deep concern. I could tell that she was unsure of whether she should stay or leave. Reluctantly, she left me alone with him and went upstairs. By the time she reached the elevator, Jeff had lost his restraint and had begun screaming at the top of his lungs. I am told that I could be heard trying to calm him.

What follows is hearsay as I have no recollection of what happened, just the aftermath. About an hour after leaving me with Jeff, Brenda came back downstairs to make sure that everything was okay. She found the apartment door ajar and let herself in. She was frightened by the scene. Everything appeared broken. Lamps were tipped over, glassware was smashed and someone had punched holes in the wall. She told me later that she feared for my life.

She heard whimpering from the rear of the apartment. Tentatively, she made her way through the battlefield that was our living room to the dim recess of our bedroom. There she found the mattress turned over and Jeff weeping, his face in his hands, repeating, "I'm sorry. I'm sorry," to a seemingly empty room.

As her eyes adjusted to the darkness, she discerned my naked figure crumpled in the corner. I was curled up into a ball, weeping, as if trying to protect myself from further assault.

"What the hell have you done?" she hissed at Jeff. She moved across the room and wrapped her arms around me.

Jeff put the bed back together and he helped me back onto it. He kept holding me and pleading for my forgiveness. I didn't speak or move. Brenda eventually went back upstairs after she felt that I was no longer in imminent danger.

The next day, Jeff treated me like a piece of fragile china. He was careful with his words and touch and offered a heartfelt apology, promising that he would never hurt me again. Together we cleaned the apartment.

Later that day, Brenda came to me when Jeff had stepped out. She was beside herself. She implored me to leave him, offering me a place to stay in her already crowded apartment. I declined, believing that Jeff's remorse and promises were real.

Tipping Point

I flew to New York to attend the Miami Project's annual dinner with my parents at the Waldorf Astoria. It had become a yearly tradition for us and I looked forward to spending time with my parents. Leaving Jeff behind felt a little like playing hooky, like I was traveling when I should have been home doing my duty. I hated the idea of the scolding and the hostility that I was going to receive on my return. I knew that there was going to be a battery of questions and taunting. He would need to make sure that I was aware of his suffering while I was away.

A lot of Miami bigwigs attend the event in New York each year. That year, six months after our initial meeting in Miami, I had the fortune of meeting up with the gentleman from the station. I was a little embarrassed that I never called him.

"I was expecting your call," he said when he saw me.

"Yeah, it's just that I've been busy with work and other things," I told him.

I made some stupid excuses and promised him that I'd call when I returned home the following week. In reality, I dreaded the idea of following up with him because I knew it would probably be a trigger for Jeff.

But New York acted like smelling salts. It put just enough distance between me and Miami for me to clear my head and acknowledge that I was in a bad situation that had to change. Being with my parents gave me a tangible reminder of my past. I had spoken to them on the phone, but to sit there and look at my mom's sweet smile as she asked me about Jeff and pretend everything was wonderful was devastating. I was embarrassed because I almost felt as if I was squandering all my parents love and care by being with him. It was an insult to their love. They had sacrificed so much so that I could live a meaningful life and here I was letting some guy demean me. Yet I felt powerless. I simply couldn't say no to Jeff. Worse still, I felt as though I *needed* him.

To realize that you feel powerless about a huge dimension of your life is a staggering moment. How could I be so weak in one area and excel in another? I was still fundraising for Project Medishare and was being headhunted by television executives. Clearly there was more out there for me than just Jeff. I made a promise to call the television station when I got back.

I returned to Miami emboldened by my positive experience in New York and ready to address matters at home. In perfect form, Jeff was a dream. He brought me flowers. He made reservations at one of my favorite restaurants. He asked about my parents. He was, generally speaking, the man I thought I had fallen in love with. I didn't mention meeting the news director that evening. I didn't want to bring up anything that might ruin the moment. After spending time with my parents and all the wonderful people from the Miami Project, I couldn't cope with any arguments. I drank my wine, ate my meal, laughed, and kept my mouth shut.

The first person I told about the news director was Brenda. She was ecstatic for me and encouraged me to check it out. Leery of Jeff, she gave me encouragement that contained a thinly veiled reference to his last outburst.

"You have to do this, Carlana. It's like a dream job," she said, "You have to think about yourself. Don't be a fool."

Her support and enthusiasm were like body armor for me. A few days later I phoned the station and made an appointment. I didn't give myself much time to lament my decision. I was to be at the station in two days and ready to meet with a variety of people, including the news director. I basked in the afterglow of the call, my mind running rampant with visions of the future. I saw myself as a reporter on the street or giving a voice and a face to the issues that had shaped my life and the lives of millions of other Americans. I saw myself making a difference and claiming a spot in the limelight.

I was so excited after the call that I couldn't focus on Haiti or anything other than looking and being my best for the people at Channel 10. I was eager to go home and watch the news. I would study the reporters to see how they dressed and composed themselves in preparation for my meeting the next day.

On the way home I picked up a bottle of wine. Even though I hadn't achieved anything yet, I felt like celebrating. I wanted to have a nice night with Jeff.

I set everything up on our coffee table, poured myself some wine, and kicked back on the couch. The news came on. Two sun-kissed faces, a man and a woman, beamed into my living room. They spoke in an upbeat singsong voice that seemed strangely out of synch with the miserable stories they were reporting. "There was a massive collision on I-95 today," one said with a saccharin smile. Fifteen minutes and another glass of wine later, I heard the sound of keys in the door. Jeff was home.

"Hi, babe," I called out to him.

"Hey."

"Want a glass 'a wine?" I asked, my Louisiana drawl stretching out the word wine like a weight tied to a rubber band.

"Sure, I'll have 'a glass of wahn," he said, mocking my southern accent. I poured him a glass, which he took with him as he walked into the bedroom to change.

"Guess what?"

"I don't guess. What is it?"

"Remember that guy from Channel 10? The one who gave me his card? I finally called the TV station today."

No response. He walked out with an empty glass and poured himself another, taking the bottle with him into the kitchen. I continued.

"I'm going down there day after tomorrow to meet with news director and see if they can use me." Still no response. "I think it's pretty exciting. Don't you?"

"Yeah, pretty cool," he said, sitting down in my wheelchair, which was parked next to the couch.

I turned my attention back to the TV and continued to drink my wine.

"So, what, do you wanna be a news anchor or something?" he said, his voice trailing off towards the kitchen.

"I dunno. I just think it's cool that they're even interested in talking to me." I watched a little longer and then my bladder started speaking to me. I needed to pee. When I looked for my chair it was no longer by the couch. I scanned the room and found it parked just outside the kitchen, which was open to the living room. I could see Jeff looking through the cabinets for something.

"Sweetie, can you bring me my chair. I gotta pee," I said, still concentrating on the TV. He didn't stop what he was doing. I waited a few minutes or so and then asked again. "Hey, I need to go. I need my chair."

I turned and saw him leaning on the counter top with one elbow and while he sipped wine out of a glass that he held in his other hand.

"Chair. Please," I said.

He just smiled. There was something eerie about him. It was no innocent smile. He smiled like a hunter who just caught his prey in a trap.

"You want to be a TV journalist. You can't even go to the bathroom without your wheelchair. Don't you think you need to be a little more resourceful than that?"

There was a tickle in the pit of my stomach.

"Just give me my chair, Jeff. I really need to go."

He pulled the chair out from wall and moved it about halfway towards me and then stopped and walked back to the kitchen.

"Come on, I made it easier. Go get it."

"Cut it out, Jeff. Just give me the damn chair."

"No."

"Jeff. Give me the goddamned chair!" I said, my eyes beginning to well up with tears.

"Why? You obviously think you can do anything."

"What do you care if I meet with the people down at the station? So what? Aren't you happy for me?"

He didn't respond and just stared at me.

"There's your stupid wheelchair. Go get it," he said, kicking it across the room and walking back to the kitchen.

I couldn't believe he was doing this to me. But I really had to go to the bathroom and couldn't wait for him to come around. Reminiscent of my days in the gym in Russia, I pulled myself off of the couch and dragged myself across the room to my chair.

"Maybe you should bring them some shots of you scurrying across the floor. That'll be real impressive."

I lifted my self up into the chair, humiliated.

"Why did you do that? What is wrong with you?" I cried.

"Do what?" he asked in a cavalier manner, taking a sip of wine.

That was it. Something in the way he said those two words flipped a switch inside me and my sadness was replaced with anger. I was ready to walk out on him right then and there. I straightened up, looked right in his eyes, and spoke my mind. "I don't know why you're so threatened by this. It's really pathetic,

Jeff. You know? Pathetic!" I turned and began to make my way towards bathroom, cursing him under my breath.

What happened next was a blur. There is almost the sensation of missing time. One moment I was rolling myself across the room towards the bathroom. I could see the doorway and the sink inside. The next I was being violently ripped out of my chair and falling fast and hard towards the floor. I landed on my hip bone and ended up crumpled on my side. Stunned, I looked up to see Jeff glaring down at me. His eyes open wide with fury. For the first time in my life, I was frightened by someone. I began to weep like a child distraught by her inability to control her environment.

"What are you doing? Please don't hurt me," I said between sobs. "I just want to go. Please just let me go."

"Pathetic! I'm pathetic? Look at you. You're a fucking cripple. You have the nerve to call me pathetic?" he shouted. He went to kick me, which I braced for, squinting my eyes and placing my hands in front of me to block him. Instead, his foot made contact with my wheelchair and it flew over onto its side.

His words that night were more damaging than his usual barbs. They were incendiary bombs aimed right at my self-esteem. All of the positive energy and hard work that I and everyone I loved—friends, parents, sisters, Saroja, and Tatiana—had tirelessly put into bridging the chasm of pain and loss that was my broken spine was challenged by his attack.

It hadn't occurred to me that I was not yet safe and secure. I didn't understand that building a bridge was one thing, yet crossing it was quite another. That letting go of my insecurities in a fundamental manner had more to do with my love for myself than another's love for me. Though it was dark and scary, that evening would be the first rocky step in my final path to freedom and self-love.

"Get the hell out then. Go," he said, as he walked out of the room and into the bedroom.

I moved quickly, dragging myself across the carpet towards my tipped-over chair and hoisting myself into it for the second time. Once in the chair, I rolled forward, grabbed my keys and purse, and made my way towards the door. I had to get out of the apartment. To get away from him. As I waited for the elevator, impatiently pressing the down button over and over, I frantically reviewed my options. *I could get in my car and go to the airport,* I thought. Once there I could call my dad and ask him to get me a ticket home to Shreveport. I would fly home and tell my parents everything. But the image of me coming into my parents' house in the middle of the night, the fugitive of a bad relationship, was too much to bear. No, I couldn't do it. I winced at idea of my telling my mother and father what had happened.

I got in my car and drove out of the parking lot. I drove with the desperate focus of a refugee fleeing a war zone, with the aching desire of an addict eager to stop participating in her own destruction. My world had finally given way. I drove towards the one piece of solid ground that remained. I drove towards Brenda.

The drive over to Brenda's house was surreal. It was dusk and the fading tropical light cast a soft glow over the city, giving it a purple and red luster. Things move slowly at that time of day, and for me the atmosphere was perfect for contemplation. It was silent, almost spiritual. It reflected the feeling of detachment that I had towards my life at that moment. And as I drove, images of my past raced through my mind: My life in Russia. My parents and sisters. All my friends from Boulder. Vast streams of time whipped through me as I tried to understand where I was and how I got there. There seemed to be a disconnect between my situation and my past, which, I felt, was marked by many successes. *This couldn't be the destination that was planned for me,* I thought. I had worked hard and overcome so much. No way. It couldn't end here.

I thought about Jeff too. I knew now that he wasn't merely hot-headed and jealous. It was clear that he had many deep-rooted and potentially volatile problems. But there was another side to him that was soft and caring and I was still able to recall the sweet, funny, and loving man that I fell in love with. I wondered if I could mend him. I wondered if perhaps I had not tried hard enough to understand him and his problems. Even after being thrown to the floor like a sack of potatoes, I was torn by my emotions. On the one hand he was my abuser. On the other, he was a human being with faults and weaknesses, just like me, crying for help.

I arrived at Brenda's apartment building, assembled my wheelchair, and got myself out of the car. I hadn't called and didn't even know if she would be there. After fumbling with the buzzer, I rang her apartment and prayed for an answer. After a moment of silence that seemed to linger for hours, there was a wonderful crackling sound followed by an inquisitive "yes?" She was home. My lifeline was home.

"It's me. Can I please come up?" I asked, in a desperate, panicked voice.

"Come up," she said into the intercom, buzzing me in immediately.

The closer I came to Brenda's apartment the more I unraveled. The detached calm with which I had driven across town was replaced by a deluge of emotions. I suppose it was the relief of reaching Brenda's apartment and the feeling that I would be, at least for the time being, safe.

Brenda was waiting for me with the door open, her body fixed against the frame. A cool breeze played with her long curly hair. Her face had the dour expression of a magistrate in an old Dutch painting. My eyes were swollen from crying. She reached out her arms and took me into them like a lost child.

"What happened?"

In the background, the phone was already ringing. It didn't take long for him to figure out my game plan.

"I need to use your bathroom," I said shakily.

"What happened?" She asked again, ready to assess as well as aid. "What did he do?" she asked.

"Mom, it's Jeff," one of her daughters said from inside.

"No!" I whispered.

"Tell him I'll call him back," she told her.

All I could do was weep. Wail actually. I wailed and wailed, unable to get any words out. I wailed until I found the breath to recall the events that had just transpired.

"You guys go to your room. Leave Carlana and Mommy alone."

Through my tear-filled eyes, I could see her two little girls standing on the other side of the room with the innocent curiosity of children bearing witness to a tragedy. They stood there silently staring, their little faces slack with uncertainty as to why an adult in their life was so out of control.

Seeing this Brenda said, "She's okay. She's just sad. Go to your room now, okay?"

For a long while I couldn't talk and simply let Brenda hold me and rub my head as I buried my face in her long curly auburn hair and convulsed in her arms. I finally broke away to use the bathroom.

When I was able to speak, it all came out in a jumbled rant.

"You know, I called like I told you I was going to. And I made the appointment for the day after tomorrow."

"The station?"

"Yea. And I got wine and everything and was feeling good. And when he came home he just freaked out."

"What did he do?"

I told her about him keeping the wheelchair from me and then picking me up and throwing me down.

She listened closely like a judge hearing a plaintiff's argument.

"I didn't know what to do. You're the only one I've got here, Bren. I think I'm leaving him. This time I think I'm really leaving him."

She nodded. "First of all, you need to break up with him. He's hurting you."

"I know," I said. "But he's not like that. This isn't really him, you know."

"No. You're wrong. This is him," she said, taking my hand in hers. "Sorry," she said, wiping my tears away with her thumb. "This *is* him."

I started to cry because even though a part of me knew she was right, I still felt for him. I couldn't just turn my feelings off and hate him, no matter what he'd done.

"I feel so stupid. It's so embarrassing," I told her.

The phone rang again.

"You're not the one who should be embarrassed," she said.

Before Brenda could pick up the receiver, her youngest, Marietta, walked out into the living room holding the cordless phone. "It's for Carlana."

"I don't want to talk to him," I whispered to Brenda.

"Give me the phone," she said sternly, taking it out of her daughter's hands and walking across the room towards the breakfast nook.

"Jeff, hi. Yes, she's here but she doesn't want to talk to you right now. Frankly, I wouldn't let her talk to you." I could hear Jeff's voice even from a distance. "It may be between you but now she's here and you're calling my phone," Brenda said defiantly. I watched her every move and tried to envision what Jeff was doing in our apartment, like the split-screen effect used in the movies. "It's a little late for that, Jeff. Don't you think?" The conversation was punctuated by pregnant pauses.

Marietta remained in the living room watching me, unable to avoid the instinctual voyeuristic magnetism of human anguish. I was a train-wreck. Ironically, I was the ten o'clock news right in her living room.

"I can hear you're upset. You should see *her*," she said glancing towards me for a moment. "I don't think it's going to do much good, but I'll tell her. No, please don't. No. Jeff, this is my house and I am asking you not to. I have two little girls here. If you come here I'm calling the police. Okay?...Okay? Yeah, bye."

She hung up and came back to the living room where I was still sitting on the couch.

"Is Carlana okay, Mom?" Marietta asked Brenda, as if I were in some other dimension beyond the logic of her world. I mulled the question over in my own mind. *No*, I thought. *No, Carlana's a fucking mess.*

"Yes, honey. Carlana's just had a fight. She is going to be okay," Brenda told her, trying to ease her concern and mine.

"With Jeff?"

"Yes."

"Did he hurt her?"

Brenda paused. "Yes, he hurt her feelings really bad," she finally said.

"I'm okay, sweet thing. I'm just a little sad and your mom's making me feel better," I said, looking at Brenda and smiling meekly.

Brenda took Marietta back to her room, put her to bed, and came out to the living room to sit with me, a single lamp lighting a small area in the otherwise dark apartment.

"What did he say?" I asked.

"He said that he wanted to talk with you. That he was sorry."

"Really? He said he was sorry?" I asked, starting to cry again. "Was he upset?" I asked.

"Yes, he was upset. Of course he was. He was upset because he was a total animal."

"He said he wanted me to call?"

"Yes. But you're not going to call are you?"

I was silent. "I have to talk to him sometime. Maybe I could use this as a chance to help him?"

"Carlana, you need to help yourself. I don't think that you should call him tonight. Let him be with himself. And don't kid yourself; he's no angel. This is just the latest. Don't you see it's getting worse, not better?"

"But if he's really sorry and understands what he's done, maybe I can help him. I think I can help him change. He just needs to understand."

"You can't help him, Carlana. He has to help himself. Isn't that what you're always telling me? That we have to be resilient and be responsible for our own lives? You can't fix him."

But I thought I could. I wouldn't tell her, but I thought that I had the capacity to take on other people's pain and help them through it. I had helped her and many other people through hard times. Why was Jeff any different? Why couldn't' I use my gift to help the man I loved change himself for the better?

"I know, but I think that he needs me," I said.

"Didn't you say once that you have to know when to let go sometimes? I think this is one of those times. You need to protect yourself."

She was throwing all my pearls of wisdom back in my face. I knew that she was right but I didn't know how to employ my own insights. I had failed myself.

"Do you think I can stay here for a while?" I asked.

She studied me for a moment. I could tell that she was choosing her words and that I might not be happy with her response.

"You can stay here, but only if you promise me something."

"What?" I asked.

"That you will never go back to him."

"We just need some time!" I said fighting back tears.

"You must understand," she said, staring unflinchingly into my eyes, "if you go to back to him, you will never be welcome in my home again."

"What do you mean? You're my best friend!" I asked, stunned.

"I am your best friend but I'm also a mom. I can't have my kids watching you. I hate to say this, but I don't want them to learn from you."

Wham! The cold hand of reality smacked me hard in the face. I think I actually felt nauseous. "I understand," I said.

"Carlana, they've seen you and Jeff fight before. Tomorrow morning they're going to wake up and see my best friend on the couch. And they're going to ask me if you and Jeff had a fight; if Jeff hurt you. They know, Carlana. They may be young but they know what's going on. If you go back again, you're setting the worst example for them. I don't want them thinking that this is normal. That his behavior is something that's acceptable. I left Puerto Rico because I wanted to give them and myself the chance of a better life and I won't let anyone get in the way of that."

"I know," I said, looking away from her. It was humiliating, but she was right. How could I, the woman who set out to be an example for people facing adversity, question her logic? If I couldn't set an example for children, what good was I?

"You're also my best friend," she continued after a moment, "and, I can't be a participant anymore. If I let you stay here and then you go home I'll be a part of your problem. I can't do that. I love you too much. Do you agree?"

I looked around. I was sitting in my best friend's apartment because my boyfriend had literally picked me up and thrown me out of my wheelchair. I was sitting there because I didn't feel safe in my own home. In this place, filled with the innocence of children and the discipline of a mother's love, the rationalizations that allowed Jeff's and my world to exist started to break down. I felt dirty. I truly was out of control. Brenda made me see that.

"Okay," I said.

And that was it. My best friend planted her foot down and said "no more." She refused to be a participant in my self-destruction. I could either quit cold turkey or stay away from her and her family. It was exactly the dose of tough love that I needed.

That night was raw and miserable, but it was my fist step towards finally letting go of the need for external validation and creating fertile ground for self-love, success, and true happiness to take root.

"Thank you. Thank you so much," I said, weeping in gratitude and, though I am loathe to admit it, sadness. Like many abused women, it was hard for me to say goodbye. To let him go for good.

Brenda went off and got pillows and blankets for me to sleep on the couch. It was still early and we sat together in the living room, talking for several more hours. She tried to drive home her belief that I was selling myself short with Jeff. That I could do much better. That I deserved better. But how could she know? She wasn't in my shoes. She didn't understand what it was like to have to roll into a bar or restaurant and have people, men and women, check you out because you were an invalid out on the town. People admired me because I defied the laws of victimhood. In my mind, they never just looked at me and said, "Gee, what a pretty girl." There was always the context, "...in a wheelchair." How could she ever know what it was like and how I felt when a man like Jeff was interested in me? He wasn't a doctor or a therapist who had grown immune to the features of paralysis. He was just a guy. Someone who most women found attractive. Brenda couldn't possibly understand.

That evening, when the lights went out, I lay alone on the couch staring at the ceiling. I thought about what had started the fight. It wasn't even a fight really. It was a fit. A rage caused by the prospect of a new career. Clearly he was threatened by the idea of me becoming a reporter. That was obvious a long time ago. But sitting there all alone, I wondered if I shouldn't have been more open with him. I really hadn't involved him in my decision. Maybe he felt insulted by my lack of consideration. Then I thought about him on the phone. He had told Brenda that he was sorry. Maybe he really was sorry.

But it was too late. I had made a promise to myself and to Brenda to get out of the situation. Just like leaving Russia, this was the right thing to do. Slowly but surely I wound my way down from the jagged emotional peaks of anger to the soft vales of nostalgia for a relationship that never really was. I wouldn't make a clean break that night, though at least I started down the path towards success.

After Brenda left for work, I took a shower and drove my apartment. It was a bit surreal driving back in the blinding daylight. The city looked so different from the night before. In the bright light of morning, the streets packed with people going about their business, the city seemed on autopilot and incapable of playing host to the kind of emotional imbroglio that occurred the night before.

I put the keys into the door with trepidation. I knew he was at work but I still felt a little uneasy. I entered the apartment and found the wine corked and on the counter by the fridge. On the coffee table was a piece of white notepad paper with a note. It said simply, "I'm sorry. I love you."

This time a note wasn't going to cut it. Brenda was right. He was getting worse. She had made many good points the night before and I kept replaying them in my head. The fact that she didn't want my problems to affect her little girls was the most telling. I was toxic. Her daughter Marietta saw right through me to my core the night before and what she saw left her confused and afraid. It was probably her first experience with an adult in emotional distress. I didn't want to be that person again.

I was uncomfortable being in the apartment and feared him returning home. I didn't know if I'd have the strength to leave if I met him there. So I gathered some clothes and headed back to Brenda's as fast as I could. I didn't even leave a note or respond to his.

I returned to Brenda and decided to call my parents. It was so hard to tell them about my situation. I was so ashamed. I almost felt like I had hurt them more than myself. They were also annoyed that I hadn't called sooner but in the end were just grateful that I had managed to get out. They made arrangements to come to Miami to spend time with me.

I spent the day watching the news and taking notes on the reporters and what kind of segments they ran. It felt good, because I could see myself doing the job. They were all like outgoing southern hostesses, even the men. Everything, no matter how tragic or fabulous, was just marvelous. In a way, they were me back in Boulder. Just put on a happy face. Hell, I had experience after all. That night I would draw upon the love and support of Brenda and her family as I readied myself for my interview the next day.

Working My Way to Sanity

My interview was a huge, potentially life-altering event. People would have killed for the opportunity that I had been given and if I slipped up in the slightest way, it would have disappeared just as suddenly as it had come. But despite my tumultuous private life, I wasn't nervous or fearful of a negative outcome at all. Out in the world, especially when it came to professional activities, my handicap had become an integral selling point. It was only in the realm of romance and relationships where my attractiveness as a woman was called into question and the chair remained a liability.

On my way to the interview I pondered the irony to the situation. I am sure that the opportunity I was given would never have come my way if I weren't in a wheelchair. I realized that my personality in juxtaposition to the chair inspired people and made me memorable. The thing that I had struggled against for so long actually made me stand out in a positive way in some forums. It made the idea of being a reporter even more precious, because it would bring more than local fame; it would allow me to help destroy the myth that those of us struck by tragedy are forever victims. That I was in the process of extricating myself from an abusive relationship, I reasoned, would be my secret.

As I entered the station that day, I didn't have the slightest doubt that the news director would fall in love with me and indeed, the meeting went very well. After the interview, he gave me a tour of the newsroom and I recognized the anchors and other reporters. The newsroom was a like a beehive. There was a buzz in the air that I found contagious. People were running around with a sense of urgency and I could see myself fitting into the scene.

When I left to go home I noticed a bunch of guys hanging around out in the parking lot talking. I said hello as I passed them and they watched as I rolled up to my car, jumped in, disassembled my wheelchair, and tossed it into the back seat, an act that I perform several times a day. As I turned the keys in the ignition and the engine turned over the men erupted into applause. It took a moment to realize that they were clapping for me. I was embarrassed at first but then I felt so proud. I waved and smiled at them. If those men only knew what that little gesture meant to me on that day.

Their applause did more than just warm my heart. It made me realize that what had become routine for me represented a significant accomplishment to most other people. It reminded me that sometimes it's important to give ourselves credit for the small victories in our lives. I tend to measure myself against major goals like job promotions and relationships. Those men made me see that even the act of putting my wheelchair in my car was something that I could be proud of. Their applause helped me to connect my past with my present. I had a momentary flashback to the night in rehab when I got myself out of bed for the first time and massaged Karen Jordan's arms. I had indeed come a long way, even if I got sidelined along the way.

I also understood that the nature of my struggle had changed. I had fought my way back from my devastating injuries to become a woman who was not afraid to take risks. It had taken some time but I had finally learned how to coexist with my arch-enemy and even leverage it to create opportunities. Something that I had tried to "fix" all these years was actually opening up doors and distinguishing me from the crowd. Now, the struggle was about being the best person I could be, regardless of whether I was sitting down or standing up. I came to Miami not knowing a single soul. Jeff was a disaster, but with the help of friends and family, I felt that I could get back on track and keep going.

Two days later I received a call from the TV station offering me the position. A new day was dawning.

Lesson Learned: *Reaching Out Is Sometimes the Best Weapon*

When I met Jeff, I had achieved academic and some professional success. I had confidence in my abilities: a confidence that spilled into other areas which were still works in progress and opened the door to the unhealthy relationship that almost consumed me.

It's important that I emphasize my participation in my abuse. It was after all a relationship. I entered into it on my own and even when the warning signs were all around me, I chose to stay. My insecurities were a critical factor in my decision to be with him and in his ability to inflict damage. I very much let him hurt me.

There are some people out there who are lucky enough to go through life without getting into dangerous situations that they can't manage alone. I think that these people are few. For the rest of us, it is important that we not be afraid to reach out when a situation becomes overwhelming. In my case, my relationship had become dangerous. Many women aren't as fortunate as me and don't ask for help in time. I was one of the lucky ones.

When I reached out for someone to help me, I didn't realize the desperate nature of my problem. It took my best friend to tell me that I wasn't in control and that I was in trouble. It took admitting that I couldn't change Jeff and that I wasn't strong enough to change my situation on my own.

Every so often, I have what I like to call a breakthrough day, a day when I know that I have changed in a positive way on a behavioral or an emotional level. Things are somehow different. I have a greater sense of control. I can feel it from the inside out. These days serve as pivotal markers for me and the day that Brenda gave me the ultimatum was one of them.

KNOW WHEN TO ASK FOR HELP

Living Proof: *Surviving Addiction*

I worked with a woman named Alice who had a twenty-three-year-old son living at home. He had been drinking and drugging since the age of fourteen. At least once a week, Alice would come in to work looking disheveled and very tired. It wasn't long before we all knew that when she looked like this, there had been trouble at home.

Her many vigorous approaches to address "the problem" had included everything from trying to talk with her son calmly to throwing him out (and then taking him back in when he made all those promises to stop). Sometimes she coped pretty well with the situation. At other times, she felt like she was going crazy and that she just couldn't do it anymore. Those were the days when she felt like her world was crashing down around her. We all know that this kind of scenario is repeated every day in millions of households, without regard to demographics, social or financial status.

Alice says she tried it all. Nothing helped. In fact, despite her best intentions and sincere attempts, things probably got worse, no matter how much Alice loved her son, no matter how much sincerity she had. She realized that she need to ASK FOR HELP.

Alice had to admit to herself that she could not rescue her son. She could be there to love and support him but she could not do the work for him. I told Alice about the many useful tools available to people like her, including understanding people who are out there and could help her along the way.

- I told her about the numerous books written for family members of drug addicts that she could find at her local bookstore, as well as numerous publications.
- I reminded her about the Internet, with its many websites, chat rooms, and facilitated discussion groups designed to help people gain a new perspective. There she could learn how others managed to conquer and emerge whole from the same stressful situation.
- I told her that there are many twelve-step recovery programs out there with stories just like hers.
- I told her that she could always choose to seek help from a professional experienced in assisting affected family members and friends, or possibly from her church.

I've stayed in touch with Alice and three years have passed since the crisis was at its peak. Alice did recognize when to ask for help. Her life has changed drastically. Mark has been attending outpatient drug counseling and has been clean and sober for two years and three months. Alice and her son have a good relationship, and in fact have opened their own business together. Alice and Mark are living proof that KNOWING WHEN TO ASK FOR HELP can change your life for the better. In their case, it even helped them survive addiction.

· EXERCISES ·

Lift me up

All of us have felt lonely, left out, or worthless due to some experience in life. In this exercise, list the feelings you have had when you were "down" for whatever reason, and put the name of a person who lifted you up and how they did it. How did they respond to your need for help? How do you think they felt about helping you? Better?

Feeling	Person & action of that person
1. _____	1. _____
_____	_____
2. _____	2. _____
_____	_____

Recognize how important it is to know when to ask for help. And remember how good it feels when you are able to help others.

. . . .

Getting out!

None of us ever want to be in an abusive relationship. However, it happens. The good news is that we can move on. This exercise involves identifying the problem and doing something about it.

If, in fact, you are currently in an abusive relationship, take action NOW! It won't get any better if you continue to stay in it. As hard as it may be, make the effort. Here is a guide:

Make a list of the possible things you can do to get out the situation and the consequences if you do them. Then, how you can overcome them:

Things I need to do	Consequences of my action
Call a counselor	*My spouse will "blow up" if I do this*

How to overcome the consequences

Don't tell my spouse
Get a friend to go with me

It sounds pretty obvious. But writing down the elements that represent the way out of difficult situations is an easy first step in taking action. It will make your exit strategy real.

CHAPTER 9

Getting Back on Track

- -

One Day at a Time

Learning that I was being offered the position at Channel 10 was a little like being alone on New Year's Eve. It was still fun and exciting, but a little empty without having someone to kiss at midnight. Even though Jeff was hostile, I was saddened by the fact that I couldn't share my success with my partner. Still, I was thrilled that I was being given an opportunity to become a television journalist, an offer that spoke to my ability as a communicator. If all went well, I would enjoy a certain amount of celebrity and have a podium to draw attention to issues that I felt were important.

I immediately gave notice at Project Medishare, an organization that I am honored to have served, informing them of my new direction. They were pleased for me and hoped that I might be able to use my newfound profession to shine a light on their cause one day.

After I received the offer I went home to Brenda's apartment, my refuge, to rejoice in the news with her and the girls. Brenda was thrilled for me, wrapping her tan arms around me and showering me with hugs and kisses. "I knew you'd get it!" she exclaimed. The kids looked at me with wide-eyed excitement that I was going to be on TV. The sentiment behind their little faces could not have been more different than the one I witnessed a few nights earlier when I showed up on their doorstep in tears.

My parents and sisters were thrilled. I phoned home as soon as I heard the news and beyond excitement, there was relief. I think that everyone close to me knew that the position represented a new focus: a way out of the darkness. Everyone, that is, except Jeff.

He was constantly phoning Brenda's house trying to reach me. His calls clogged the answering machine and my voice mail at work. A couple of days after showing up at Brenda's, I had the first of many desperate and often angry phone exchanges that tested my nerves. He tried to convince me to give the relationship another shot, saying things like, "Can we please try again?" "I have a temper, but you know I love you," "I promise I won't ever hurt you again," and, "I'm sorry. I just lost it." They were statements that have all become part of our collective vernacular due to the many films and programs that deal with the issue of domestic abuse.

I tried to talk with him, to communicate how much he hurt me. I tried to explain "why," but in the end my response was always simple and unrelenting: "Jeff, I can't stay with you anymore. I just can't," and then finally, "I'm sorry."

He was angry and hurt and I would by lying if I said I was completely confident in my decision to leave him. I still wasn't over him in my heart, even after all the ridicule and abuse. But with Brenda's help, I knew I would find the strength to move forward.

I would learn over the next several months that getting out of a bad relationship is often a little like quitting smoking. Few people manage to quit cold turkey. You slowly taper off until one day you realize you don't need the fix anymore. It is longer still until you are disgusted by the idea of cigarette. The same went for my relationship with Jeff. Though I left him physically, we would continue to talk with one another for months before I would finally close the door forever. In the time in between, I poured myself into my new career. It was this new focus and the lessons and victories that came with it that served as a ladder to solid ground.

Using the Chair to My Advantage

Accepting the position at Channel 10 was not an express ticket to local stardom. In concept I was embarking on a glamorous new career in television news. In reality I had left a good job with a comfortable salary at Project Medishare for a trainee position with no guarantees of a payout of any kind. I was not much more than an intern and had to change the way I lived my life dramatically. And believe me, after being in charge of my little operation and hosting glamorous events it wasn't the easiest segue. Staying at Brenda's took a lot of the emotional strain out of my transition because she and the kids were so supportive.

In many ways I was beginning again. I was rebuilding myself from the ground up and in the process finally fixing the weaknesses that allowed Jeff to happen (I often find myself talking about him like a category five hurricane). For that reason alone, I was willing to sacrifice my comfort in the short term and press on with my life. Even after Jeff, and perhaps because of him, I refused to let go of the vision that I had of myself back in high school. I wouldn't let that brave little girl die and I believed with all my heart that I was put here to do something special, that I was given my challenges for a reason and it was my responsibility to overcome them and see it all through. I still felt certain that something big was waiting for me.

My early days at the station were all about learning the trade—getting down and dirty in the field doing the set-up for other reporters. It was not glamorous stuff. There were long hard days of me going out on location with a camera crew to interview people in preparation for someone else's story.

One of the things that I leveraged early on as a reporter most was, ironically, my wheelchair. I would roll up and ask people if they had a moment to chat in my most perky southern accent. It's very hard to say no to a girl in a wheelchair holding a microphone.

The chair created an immediate intimacy between me and the people I met because it was a huge aspect of my physicality and it laid my adversity bare for everyone to see. It told people that I was flawed. When I was talking to someone who had suffered, I think that it created the expectation that I could empathize with their struggles because I had waged my own battles. On the other hand, my attitude and presence told them that I was a survivor and not a victim and that put them at ease while it gave them comfort and inspiration. As a result, people opened up to me very easily. I ended up getting the best background interviews for other reporters' stories. I even got big burly truckers to stop and smile and give me a sound bite, holding my microphone as high as possible so that they could talk from an open window in their rigs.

After I was finished, the reporter would show up and I would hand over my material and watch as they reported live from the scene. It was all work and no glory. But I was like a sponge, taking in as much as I could at every moment.

The frenetic nature of the work was also a welcome distraction from Jeff. I was so busy that I often didn't have time to think about anything except getting my assignments to the producers on time. He was still very much with me though, and he would make his presence known when I started showing up on the nightly news.

My very first on-air moment came a couple months after I joined the station. I was to report on the Big Brothers/Big Sisters programs in South Florida. My job was to interview a little girl and her big sister to promote participation in the program. The girl was terribly shy and I did everything short of hiring a clown to get her to open up. I love kids and she was very sweet, but her shyness was jeopardizing my report. It took a ride in the news truck, a bowl of ice cream, and serious swing time in a local park to get her to talk. Inside, I was screaming with the earnestness of a vaudevillian ringmaster, *Come on, kid! You're on!* I fantasized about getting Brenda's daughter to do a stand-in but eventually, while sitting on the park swing, she smiled and said that she loved her Big Sister just like a real sister. That was it, my big shot and my first on-air success. It would lead to me getting my own weekly franchise called Wednesday's child.

That first story set the tone for the early phase of my career. They used me to cover soft news and especially any story that involved a physical handicap. Whenever something was happening at the Miami Project, I was there to get the news. If a local paraplegic did good, enter Carlana Stone. It would have been fine if it had been one facet of my job, but it felt like those were the only stories that the editors thought were appropriate for me. Wheelchair-bound girl covers wheelchair scene. Frankly, it was all a bit too predictable.

I totally understand their rationale, but I wanted to be seen as a reporter who just happened to be in a wheelchair. I knew, though, that I would have to endure typecasting until I learned the ropes and earned people's respect. Don't get me wrong, there were amazing moments for me during those first few months. I interviewed people like James Brady, Ronald Reagan's press secretary who was shot during the assassination attempt, and was honored to be out there giving a human face to important social issues. Still, I wanted more. Thankfully, someone else at the station believed in me and would help me break away from covering stories about people with disabilities. He saw in me a real talent to be a human interest reporter.

Thank God for Advocates

Sometimes we are lucky enough to have advocates in life. They might appear in the workplace or in school or in whichever forum we are trying to make our way. I had one at Channel 10.

A typical day in news begins with what are called pitch meetings, where people get around a table and pitch story ideas for that day's news coverage. At one of these meetings, it was decided that I would cover Barbie's newly released handicap friend. It seemed that Mattel released the toy while Barbie's house was still inaccessible to wheelchair-bound dolls. I will never forget when our general manager, John Garwood, marched into our pitch meeting one day and declared that I would not be covering any more handicap stories. He always went to bat for me. He shared my vision; he recognized my potential and made sure that I was given the opportunity to grow. I can honestly attribute my success in Miami and beyond to his early confidence and support.

After Garwood mandated that I be given real news stories to cover, life at Channel 10 changed dramatically. I was suddenly out there covering stories about the major issues and people making an impact in the Miami area. Just a few months into my one-year training program, I was quickly earning a name for myself at the station and gaining the respect of my colleagues and producers.

I have to mention how important it was to have the support of Brenda and her children during this period. I am forever indebted to them. Very few of us get through life without falling down once or twice. Besides giving me shelter, they shared in my victories. The kids were old enough to understand that it was unique to be on television and they were excited to be seen with me in public. Their pride was infectious and it helped to heal my wounded ego and build my self-esteem. Their presence would be critical in my effort to keep Jeff at bay.

Unfortunately, the more I showed up on television the more Jeff began to pester me. It began as a trickle. A call here or there. But it eventually became an unrelenting assault and on some days, when I felt down, he would whip me backwards in time, stirring up old feelings and opening up old wounds.

It was nerve-racking and embarrassing. I worked around people who made their careers by sniffing out stories and it didn't take an investigative journalist to recognize that there was something ugly about the calls that I was receiving. People would look at me through the corners of their eyes as I tried to conduct my conversations with him in hurried whispers. They would see the pain in my face afterwards and, on occasion, the tears that I tried to hide by rushing to the restroom and dabbing my eyes until I pulled myself together. Eventually, I let some people in on the saga. It was a huge release to finally share my dark secret and everyone I told could not have been more supportive.

When I look back, I feel it's no surprise that Jeff stepped up his antics as my world was coming together. With time and the perspective that it afforded me, his calls made my culpability in my own abuse that much more obvious and intolerable. I was growing more defiant in my attitude towards him and he could tell that I was slipping out of his reach. He knew that it was only a matter of time before I would turn my back on him forever and deny him completely, when I would finally say "no."

For a while, however, I continued the cycle of abuse by continuing to take his phone calls. He would sometimes phone ten or twenty times a day and I was compelled to answer the phone. One day he called just before I went on location with a camera crew to tape a report. I don't recall where I was going. When I got into the news van I was shaking and visibly distraught. I had worked with one of the cameramen before but wasn't especially close to him. His name was JP. He asked me what was wrong and I gave him the abridged version of my personal life.

I told him, "I can't believe this has happened to me. I'm the strongest person I know. I've been through so much!"

His reply was as profound as it was nonchalant, "Maybe you're not as strong as you think you are."

His words were an epiphany. It was the first time someone had suggested to me that perhaps, just perhaps, my skin wasn't as thick as I had imagined. This may sound unbelievable given my relationship with Jeff, but up until that time in my life I believed that I could handle anything because I had overcome my disability in so many tangible ways. Part of my healing was being able to accept that I was a person with flaws and weaknesses. To fully acknowledge them and understand them. Again, it was about learning how to come to terms with the world *inside*.

Going for It

Over time I began to reconnect with the path that I had started down in Russia, the optimistic path that gave me the strength to choose challenge over comfort. I continued on my way towards true self-sufficiency, which for me meant much more than being able to pay my own bills. For me self-sufficiency was not needing to look outside of myself for validation as a person and as a woman. The more time I spent as a single adult woman and the more distance there was between me and my life with Jeff, the more I learned how to embrace myself. I liked receiving praise, still do, but I was finally learning how to feel good without it.

More basic than that, I was finally letting myself begin to grieve my loss. Once I started feeling my way through the world rather than just blasting through headfirst, I learned to trust myself again because I understood myself more fully than I ever had before. Being in touch with my feelings was painful at times, but it was empowering. As a result, I began to assert myself in ways I never had imagined.

We have all heard the stories of successful people who threw caution to the wind and seized an opportunity that gave them visibility and helped them pull ahead of the crowd. Many professional people have been faced with a chance to distinguish themselves early on in their careers. Often times these chances involved huge risk. Several months after arriving at Channel 10, I was faced with such an opportunity. Looking back, it took a lot of guts to do what I did but it was a gamble that paid off.

I was at Channel 10 in the mid to late nineties, arriving not long after the first Gulf War. At the time, General Norman Schwarzkopf was still very much in the news and quite a celebrity. He had a reputation in the news business as being rather ornery when it came to the press (sorry, General). In fact, it was common knowledge that he was not very keen on reporters at all and to land a story with him was, for any journalist, a major coup.

I had known that the general was involved with the Miami Project. He had been active with them in terms of fundraising and had publicly supported their activities. It speaks for the man, since he is in a profession where paralysis is an accepted on-the-job risk. Someone at the Miami Project told me that he was coming to town for an event and I made a few phone calls and managed to land an exclusive with him. In news, you quickly learn how to use your resources to your benefit. I was thrilled, because an interview with Schwarzkopf was going to mean ratings for Channel 10 and notoriety for me. I saw this as my chance. It was an opportunity for me to land a world-class interview and also to break away from the handicap genre once and for all.

When I approached my news director he was thrilled. Somewhere in the excitement of the moment I informed him that I wanted to cover the piece on air. The enthusiasm left his face and he became quite serious, exclaiming that I would have to give the piece to a seasoned political correspondent. He just didn't think I was ready.

I recall the moment vividly. I was faced with a choice: agree to go along with my boss and the person who had given me many opportunities or fight for what I believed was rightfully mine. In the end I decided to stiffen my spine and stand my ground. It was my contact after all, and I was the one who landed the story; I was holding the ropes to the interview. With as much confidence as I could muster I told our news director that either I be allowed to conduct the interview myself or he didn't get the story.

I can only imagine what must have been going through that poor man's mind. Here was the junior reporter, the sweet little girl in the wheelchair, extorting his blessing. He was clearly annoyed and stunned at my chutzpa. But there must have been admiration and respect too, because after much haggling he agreed. I was thrilled for having landed the interview and for having stood up for myself.

Over the next day or so I learned the details of his visit and determined how we would approach the general and conduct the interview. I learned that he was going to be traveling to Tallahassee to urge the state government to allocate funding for the Miami Project. Thus the interview carried professional and personal significance for me. He would fly to the state capital from Miami on a private plane and it was decided that I would ride along with him and conduct the interview upon arrival.

The plane was a plush Gulfstream G-4, a luxurious private jet. When we boarded the plane, Schwarzkopf hadn't arrived. I was carried on and placed on the couch inside. My chair was put away. Schwarzkopf boarded a few minutes later and he had his arm in a sling, which I would later learn was caused by a shoulder injury. We were introduced but he had no idea that I was in a wheelchair because he hadn't seen me board the plane and nobody from the Miami Project had informed him. He only knew that I was from the media and he hated the media. We got off to a rocky start and he ignored me for most of the trip.

When we arrived in Tallahassee and everyone proceeded to get off the plane, he, like a true gentleman, said, "Ladies first." It was then that I told him that I had to wait for my chair. He balked and said, "You've got to be kidding me!" I suppose he respected me more because I was suddenly speaking from the trenches. I had credibility and I would like to think that, in a way, maybe he felt that I was a soldier just like him. After that moment, he didn't leave my side. He was my new best friend and he gave me a great interview. A few years later, I interviewed him again and then, once I decided to come to Los Angeles, he wrote a letter on my behalf to help me land a job with King World. He's a good man.

The interview with Schwarzkopf was a huge turning point in my career. I demonstrated that I could tackle big names and handle world-class interviews. My managers had a newfound respect for me. I was no longer just a trainee. I had proven that they could trust me with important stories and bank on me to grow into to a great reporter.

The interview also marked a rise in my local celebrity. People began to recognize me around town, in the grocery store, in bars, in restaurants. It felt funny, losing some of my anonymity, but it was also enjoyable. You can't help but feel important when the checkout girl looks at you and pauses before asking, "Aren't you on the news?" You feel like you're making a difference.

One afternoon, a lady approached me in the library. I was researching a story there and she came up and grabbed my arm. She was plainly dressed and a bit worn for her years. She looked at me and in a soft voice, trying not to bring attention to herself said, "Our group talks about you." It was a bit odd. But she went on to tell me that she was a recovering heroin addict and was part of a support group that met weekly. Apparently they were using me as an example of what was possible in life if you put your mind to something. They had talked about me overcoming obstacles and felt that if I could learn to cope with life in a wheel-chair well enough to land a position on a major news station, they could overcome their addictions. I had been an inspiration to them. She honestly told me that I had helped to save her life. The moment left me dazed. I took her hand in mine and pulled her close for a hug and offered a heartfelt thank you. It was an amazing day. I don't even know her name. I didn't tell her that I was in the process of overcoming a kind of addiction of my own.

Moments like that are rare. We all do things to help others at some point in life. But to have a stranger tell you that you saved them is life-altering. It is one of my most poignant memories and probably one of the greatest honors that I will ever enjoy. It was also a valuable source of inspiration at a time when I needed to feel good about myself. The woman in the library couldn't know how her words would help push me forward. How, ironically, she would play a small role in my eventual passage from darkness to light.

I started to use my celebrity as a tool. I volunteered in schools, speaking to high school students about the dangers of drinking and driving. I was a warning as well as a source of inspiration. I wondered, looking in the crowd, which one of those fresh faces was dealing with abuse at home or at the hands of a partner. Perhaps some of them were into drugs or might one day be in a chair, just like me. I showed them that just because they may be faced with an adversity, they didn't have to give in. They could still pursue their dreams and aspirations.

Connecting the Dots

Several months after leaving him, I finally stopped speaking with Jeff altogether. It took restraining orders to keep him at bay and a lot of perseverance, but I did it. I didn't do it alone. In the end I got back on my feet with the assistance of friends and family. Brenda was my rock throughout my entire stay in Miami. She was a witness to my lowest moments and a cheerleader when I began to turn my life around. And she was by no means my only savior. The station's general manager eventually gave me an advance that enabled me to move out on my own. You just don't forget things like that. I was humbled and inspired by the generosity of the people in my life and by my own resilience. I had survived, what remains for me, my darkest days.

Day by day, through reporting, public speaking, and just spending time with myself, I made my way out of the disorienting emotional whirlpool that was my relationship with Jeff. The more victories I experienced at the station, earning people's respect as a reporter, the better I felt about myself. There was no magic involved. I built a foundation one piece at a time, success by success, and slowly reclaimed my life.

One of the most important exercises that helped me was to trace my emotional history in an effort to understand how I dealt or didn't deal with events in my life. Of course, it all came back to the accident. Nearly twelve years had passed. The farther away in time that you get from an event, the more you forget the context. I had lost the use of my legs at seventeen, an age marked by sexual awakening and an overwhelming need to be accepted by our peers. For most, hopefully, that need is tempered over time as they grow as individuals. My growth, however, took a different course.

In my effort to heal, I focused on the physical. My arms grew strong and powerful and I was able to compensate for my loss: I drove a car, skied, skydived, and was able to maneuver my wheelchair almost anywhere. People saw a young woman who seemed unstoppable. On the inside, however, I had avoided rehab, choosing to dodge my fears and insecurities rather than face them head-on the way I did my physical challenges.

When James, my boyfriend at the time of the accident, stopped calling me, I felt abandoned, no longer viable. For me, my greatest insecurities centered around my attractiveness as a woman. My love-ability if you will. Not until Saroja, years later, did I experience an intimate relationship. And being with Saroja was somehow different than being with the men at home. I don't want to discount my time with him in any way. However, it was a relationship that existed under unique circumstances. In Russia I felt special. My passport and relative affluence compensated for my flaws, real and perceived. Back on my home turf, I felt just as unlovable as before.

Because of this, I was vulnerable to people and situations that fed my latent need for attention and approval. It was almost as if a part of my development was frozen in time. In some ways, I was still a seventeen-year-old looking for the approval of her peers. Despite all of the pain, Miami freed me from this mental trap and marked the beginning of a long period of personal growth.

I was more centered and had developed a keen awareness of my deep-rooted need for validation. I knew that I had to be wary of that weakness as I moved forward.

Turning the World on Its Head: The Tatiana Factor

On a more pragmatic level, I was no longer focusing my energy on trying to free myself from the chair and denying its role in my life. I stopped looking for miracle cures once and for all and totally accepted that I would be sitting down for the rest of my life. Indeed, I realized that I was able to leverage my wheelchair in certain professional circumstances to my advantage. That represented a great deal of progress from the days of total avoidance in college.

Once I tasted my potential through my work as a reporter, I saw a great future. In terms of my career, specifically a life in the media, the chair set me apart: it would be my costar. It had taken a long time, but the thing that I had tried to escape all these years was now actually opening up doors and distinguishing me from the crowd.

We all have external attributes that, at least initially, shape people's perception of us. I often hear, "I don't think of you as being in a wheelchair," or "I don't see you as handicapped." What do those statements mean exactly? They tell me that people have built-in expectations or prejudices of what a person in a wheelchair should be like. When I fail to conform to their expectations, I rock their world. When I come into a room wearing a provocative outfit, my Louisiana accent piercing the air, heads turn. If you are dealing with a visible handicap like I am, those are two basic qualities that people find arresting. My advice: be smart about it. How we choose to act vis-à-vis the perceived attributes can make us or break us.

Emboldened by my professional success in Miami and by the boost of confidence that came from freeing myself from Jeff, I began to dream big. I felt as if I had been given an opportunity and I wanted to run with it. Being a regular on the news in Miami was fabulous. But I saw myself doing much more. I saw myself becoming a major media personality.

For me there was only one place on the planet where I could achieve my dreams: Hollywood. So, like countless starry-eyed hopefuls all over the world, I said my goodbyes, packed up my life, and headed to Southern California.

Leaving Jeff was by far the hardest thing I've ever had to do. So deep was my insecurity in terms of my worth as a woman that when I left I thought I might be alone forever. Understanding what enabled me to end up in such a destructive environment, to run so amuck, was critical to my being able to move on. Once I admitted and understood my weaknesses, I was less vulnerable to them. Honesty to oneself really is power.

Up until Miami, I had processed my world on an intellectual level. I was able to identify goals, establish a strategy, and work steadily towards them. Even if the goals reflected immense emotional issues, I never addressed them directly. If I acted the part of the unbeatable survivor, I reasoned, my emotional reality would follow. Life is not so simple.

For example, in Boulder, my goal was peer acceptance—not unusual for college-aged men and women. However, my strategy involved denying the pain surrounding my loss through total avoidance of the subject. I kept myself and others focused on anything but my paralysis. The strategy reflected my underlying insecurity regarding my attractiveness and desirability. While my actions endeared me to many, they didn't address the flaws in my character that made me so desperate for approval. I was not honest with myself. Jeff was a symptom of my underlying flaws and was enabled by my dishonesty.

This is not a black and white situation. It is not as if, emotionally speaking, there was total darkness before Miami and light after. Every year I learned more truths. I witnessed firsthand how successful people manage to overcome huge burdens by being solid in their belief in themselves and by understanding what really matters to them. These were cognitive leaps that helped me to achieve great successes. However, it wasn't until I was honest with myself that I was truly empowered and able to move forward with confidence and insight.

EMPOWER YOURSELF WITH THE TRUTH

Living Proof: *Surviving Bulimia*

When we avoid pain, what we are really avoiding is the act of grieving. In my case, I grieved for my body, my past, and my future. I grieved for my family. But grief can be dangerous if it is not tapped into and allowed to run its course. Sometimes it can build like steam in a pressure cooker until it becomes a force for destruction. Tucker and his drug abuse were a testament to that.

This notion reminds me of a lady I met at a weekend retreat where I shared my story. She turned to me in a desperate cry for help. I'll call her Sarah.

You see, in high school, Sarah liked to drink. Adding to her complexity, she was a bulimic, something with which she struggles to this day. She told me that her bulimia was the only thing in her life over which she felt she had control. As she grew older, she confided, it became painfully clear that her problems were taking over her life. During her teen years, she would drink to the point of silliness, yet as she settled into her twenties and thirties, she routinely drank to the point of blacking out. She, like Tucker, masked the pain. And worse, she was now fighting a losing battle with bulimia. The bulimia was now controlling her. And rather than reaching out for help, she began to withdraw, sharing less and less of herself with the people who cared for her the most.

It is difficult to be in a situation where a loved one is displaying self-destructive warning signs. It is often easier to play by their rules and avoid the issue out of awkwardness and perhaps even out of respect for one's privacy. During that weekend retreat I shared Tucker's story and how I earned his confidence and trust. It took some time, even with me, one of his best friends, but eventually he was able to reveal himself and it was liberating for him. I discovered that he was abused as a child. At that weekend retreat, Sarah confided in me that she, too, had been abused as a child. She had carried all of the guilt into her adulthood and it haunts her to this day. She never shared exactly how, but it was there, that same sadness that consumed Tucker. But once she was able to open up, she no longer had to assume that burden alone. And it was there that her healing began.

I do know that her abuse went far beyond the physical. She dealt with threats, insults, and criticisms—emotional abuse that tore this young lady down to the core, and destroyed any possibility for her to believe in herself. She was frequently told she was crazy. She suffered from a poor self-image and very low self-esteem. Emotional scars oftentimes last longer and carry more significance than the physical ones. The cuts heal, the bruises fade, and broken bones mend. But the ugly words that bounce around inside your head oftentimes never leave you.

I didn't cure Sarah or make all the pain go away, but once she told me there was a visible sense of relief in her eyes and one could even sense a change in the way she held herself—her stature was more confident. I would find that she feared her wounds had corrupted or spoiled her in some way and she feared that those whom she had invited into her painful world would ultimately reject her. I was able to help her carry the load just by my knowing the truth. I urged her to seek professional help and she did.

Over the years, she's had many highs and lows. For Sarah, depression was, at first, a constant companion. She enabled her own misery by continuing the cycle of binging. Some days, she told me, it was a struggle just to get out of bed. She began to talk about her fears and share her problems with the people that loved her, as well as with therapists. But once she began to let herself acknowledge and work through her pain by sharing it with others, she began to make different choices.

Today, after a lot of hard work, Sarah's married to a man who treats her with love and respect. For the first time in her life, she is able to stand naked in front of another human being with her shame and insecurities exposed. Like me in Boulder, she, in the beginning, worried that her husband would be repulsed by her. She had been a woman who mistrusted the world because of the injustices that she experienced as a child. But in the end she found hope in the potential of others and an optimism that she had never known.

Sarah is living proof that our lives take on new meaning once we empower ourselves with the truth behind our own pain and suffering.

Purging the right stuff

If you are a bulimic, then you are binging and purging. And in order to stop and save yourself, you must stop what you are doing. That means finding other things to do instead of binging.

Make a daily journal and write down five to ten things in your life that are positive. Go to the store and buy a magazine. When you get home, go through the ads, articles and photos. Tear out everything that promotes thinness or unattainable bodies. Include thin models, ads for weight loss, and ads for plastic surgery. How much of the magazine is left? Take all of the pages that you have torn out and form a pile. Tear the junk pile to shreds. And whenever you have a negative thought today, write it down, then tear up the paper. Replace the thought with a positive one!

· · · ·

Games people play

What games have you played? Can you identify them? List at least seven. Example: *I'm doing GREAT!* (at the same time, you're not...lying to others and to yourself)

Which ones of them are you still playing? Be honest and determine what you need to do to stop playing, w here you're not being honest with yourself. Decide on a plan of action and commit to it.

CHAPTER 10

Putting It All on the Line

· ·

Los Angeles: A Garden in the Desert

The approach by car into Southern California from the east is marked by mile after mile of parched desert. Endless planes of scrub brush dotted with small eroded mountains and hills painted in the red and brown tones of exposed minerals. The land is infertile and it is hard to imagine that the country's second largest metropolitan area lies somewhere ahead, just over the towering San Bernardino Mountains.

The landscape was a perfect metaphor for my personal struggle up until that point. The accident, like a bomb, rendered my young worldview a desert. It wiped away all of the traditional things that gave my life color and meaning. Sports, the simple pleasures of walking and running, and my sense of attractiveness were gone in an instant, the latter proving to be the most disabling as I grew older.

Now thirty, I had spent the last thirteen years trying to overcome the physical loss and rebuild my life through pure gumption and the insights gained from others. Karen Jordan in rehab, Tucker and the kids in Boulder, Tatiana and Saroja in Russia, and Brenda in Miami; all of these people had imparted me with wisdom. And since I had experienced many wonderful things on my journey through life up until Miami, I assumed that I had found my way back and repaired the damage caused all those years before. But Miami taught me that my emotional landscape remained a desert, and that my positive experiences were like oases, where, while inside and enjoying their life-giving properties, it was easy to forget the harshness of the land around them.

So on I drove, empowered by the lessons learned during my fall into despair, armed by a better understanding of my flaws and what prevented me from creating a lush landscape rather than isolated gardens. This time, I was ready to make hard decisions and be honest with myself, even if it meant loneliness and pain, so that hope, satisfaction, and true self-confidence could finally take root and flourish.

When I finally rounded the last set of mountains and entered the Los Angeles basin, I felt invigorated by the verdant landscape and the energy that seemed to grow as the freeway grew wider and more and more people charged their way into the city. The freeways, which would become my nemesis in the years to come, were like arteries on that day, pumping new arrivals and resident dreamers relentlessly forward.

But the landscape resonated with me. Here desert was transformed into fertile land. This was the place for me. A city founded by stubborn visionaries and powered by the whimsical musings of people who dare to dream big.

Reconnecting with Old Friends

I made my way to Marina Del Ray. I would initially stay with Pete and Ed, two college friends of mine from Boulder. These two guys had an apartment on the beach and I was graciously awarded couch space until I could get on my feet and find my own place. It was just before the huge real estate boom that would drive up prices in the Marina and make beachfront rentals a luxury for young bachelors like them.

Back in Miami, I had been living in a house with two young kids and before that with Jeff, who, despite all his shortcomings, kept a clean house. I absolutely adored these guys (still do), but I was a bit unprepared for the LA bachelor pad that would become my temporary home.

It wasn't that there was garbage strewn about, but it definitely gave me a flashback to my dorm room in Boulder. It had that well-partied-in kind of feel and a patina caused by endless smoking, drinking, and eating on the couch. I had the feeling that if you placed a section of the couch underneath a microscope you might find entire civilizations of complex organisms living off the detritus of two male twenty-somethings.

It was nice to see them though, especially after the long drive and everything that had happened in Miami. During the last year I had cut myself off from many friends. Pete and Ed were a thread to Boulder, a pleasant period in my life. And they were old friends who embraced my new dream of becoming a media personality as if it was their own.

"Yeah, come on man, you've got the moxie to do it," Pete would say, taking a puff off his cigarette and cracking open a beer. He was a struggling musician who had dreamed of being a rock star since high school. He was, and still is, a talented musician and plays a mean bass for several bands. "You just gotta really want it."

Ed was a cocky little SOB that I had a crush on in college. He's a clever guy who always manages to have fun and turn a profit at the same time. He loved to dive and found a way to make money by becoming a film production specialist for aquatic scenes. He can be a merciless wit and then the first one at your door when he hears you're in trouble. He called me Lana.

The beach was literally right across a narrow street that was used mainly by residents. It wasn't like I was going to be rolling across the sand but it was nice to know that the blue Pacific (or dark green, depending on the day and the location) was just a hundred yards away.

I called Brenda during those early days. I missed her so much.

"I can't believe I'm really here," I'd say.

"You're gonna kick butt," she'd tell me.

On a clear day I could see a dab of white on the hills to the east. Even from a distance, I knew what it was: the Hollywood sign. It hung over the city in bold relief against the green hillside. A few days after my arrival I would make way towards it and, like so many prospectors before me, try to stake my claim.

The Dream Machine Up Close

Hollywood. It looms large in the American psyche. More than a city lying a few miles north of downtown Los Angeles, it is a seductive temptress that draws people from all over the country and beyond. Its personality is complex: It is fast-talking politician and philosopher; glamorous goddess and gluttonous ogre; it is unbound riches and desperation; embracing warmth and bitter rejection. Exactly which face of Hollywood one sees, I believe, depends on the person. In a way, your fate is in your own hands. Thus, it is critical that you know your flaws before you arrive, as Hollywood will surely sniff them out and use them against you.

It's common knowledge that Hollywood is a town built on facades and values the goddess above all. We've all seen the lovelies sashaying down the red carpet at the Oscars. If you are, like me, someone who suffers from an insecurity that has its roots imbedded in your sense of attractiveness...beware. The town can make you feel less than human if you don't look like the people in the spotlight. I would have to manage this in the beginning. However, I was sure of myself in terms of my abilities and talents and that would be my saving grace.

Riding into Hollywood for the first time is exciting. All the landmarks and signage provide a sensory feast and confirm that you have actually landed in the storied city. The busy intersection of Hollywood and Vine and the fantastical architecture of Grauman's Chinese Theater evoke the golden age of film. Driving down Hollywood Boulevard as a new arrival and seeing all those stars on the sidewalk, you can't help but imagine that one day you might have one of your own. There are those lucky few after all, and during those first few days and months, before you have the chance to fathom the scope of the competition and it's all still fresh, you can almost feel the glow of stardom.

I arrived, like many before me, with a vision. I saw myself as a trailblazer, a ready pioneer in the genre of talk TV. I knew that I had a presence. I had been "discovered" in Miami after all. I had experience producing stories for TV news and knew what it was like to be in front of the camera. I also had a wonderful letter of endorsement from "Stormin'" Norman Schwarzkopf to Michael King, one of the heads at King World Productions. In this regard, I was way ahead of the many who show up without knowing a soul and whose closest connection to the entertainment business is a defining moment in a movie theatre that leaves them transfixed, inspired, and riding a Greyhound Bus west.

To me, my experience in Miami, both professionally and personally, was a Cinderella story that set me apart from the crowd. I felt that I was worthy of the attention and respect of studio executives. I had gone from victim to survivor, fundraiser to reporter, all while sitting down in a wheelchair. Also, I didn't want to act. I wanted to become an Oprah or an early Katie Couric. And, I was...in a wheelchair! There hadn't been anyone yet who could sit down with guests, look them in the eye and say, "I understand what it feels like to struggle. You can talk to me." The world was ready for someone like me. I had credibility and a reel of tape to prove it. I would be the first.

Unfortunately, I found that being a small-time news reporter from Miami was about as influential as doing a tap dance outside of a talent agent's office. I had learned the names of several studios producing good talk TV and had done some additional digging to find out who was in charge. But I decided I would waste no time and play the most logical and only card in my deck: my letter from the general to Michael King.

One morning during my first week or so in Los Angeles, I made my way over to King World in Santa Monica. It's an old studio harking back to the early days of Hollywood and still going strong. I rolled into the executive offices completely unannounced and introduced myself to the receptionist as a "friend of Schwarzkopf" who was interested in speaking with Michael King. Before she had a chance to respond, to shoot me down, I drew out my letter of recommendation like a gunslinger in the Old West and scored a direct hit.

The combination of wheelchair, southern sweetness, and a general's endorsement thwarted any effort on her part to have me expelled from the office. She relented. She just didn't have the heart to tell a young woman in a wheelchair to hit the road, so she let me hang out. I am sure that if I had been able-bodied they would have called security and had me escorted out of the building immediately. I'm also sure that somewhere in the back of her mind she feared pissing off Norman Schwarzkopf. No one, not even heartless Hollywood receptionists, care to be on the receiving end of a phone call from a barking mad general. One can only imagine, "You threw that little girl out? Put Michael on the phone!"

She marched off to see if Michael would see me and returned empowered yet not completely sure of herself.

"He's really busy right now," she said, handing me back the letter.

"Can I wait?"

"It's going to be a while."

"No problem, I can wait. I won't even bother you. I'll wait outside in the foyer. I'll be as quiet as a mouse," I said.

She must have appreciated my gumption, because she looked at me, surrendered a little smile, and said she'd keep me posted.

Meanwhile, out in the foyer I was like Lucy in one of her Hollywood episodes. I yapped with everyone who walked by. For all I knew they were all heavy hitters and decision makers. I drank coffee and kept my eyes peeled. It's pretty hard to ignore a young woman in a wheelchair and soon the people who worked there became spectators in my attempt to get in to see Michael.

"Not yet?" they'd say with smile after passing me during the first couple hours and then, "You're still here!" in amazement as morning passed into afternoon.

"Still here," I'd say, wired on coffee, trying not to wilt. Sometime around three or four in the afternoon I was informed that there would be no meeting. When I asked about the next day, I was told something like, "You can try." I called it a day and went home to Pete and Ed's that night discouraged but undeterred.

Pete was my husky cheerleader. "This is what it's all about, man. You gotta just go after it." And he was absolutely right.

The next day I drove back over to Santa Monica and rolled into Michael King's office prepared for another stakeout. To my relief, the vigil paid off and before I even had a chance to have a second cup of coffee, I was led back into his office and into my very first Hollywood pitch meeting. It would be the first time I would share my vision with someone who had the power to make it happen.

I told him how I knew the general and why I had come to speak with him. He was very cordial and chuckled when I told him that I was going to be the next Oprah. I begged him to take a chance on me and he took me around the studio to meet some of his most important television producers. I let them know that I was also interested in working on a show to see how things were done behind the scenes and played up my story-producing experience in Miami. There was nothing really there for me and it ended up being nothing more than a VIP studio tour, but I had met some very powerful people and made a positive impression. It helped make my dream that much more real. Who knew what might come of it?

Over the next few days I puttered around Hollywood trying unsuccessfully to get in to see a few other big names. The initial euphoria of being on the fringe of greatness began to wear off after a few weeks and I turned my focus on more practical and immediate ambitions: home and finances.

West Hollywood: A Stop on the Yellow Brick Road

As much as I loved staying with the boys, I realized that I needed to find my own apartment as soon as possible. It was important if I was to start growing roots and make Los Angeles home. Getting an apartment would seal my commitment to my professional goal. Besides, I wanted to stand on my own two feet and was actually looking forward to spending time alone in my own four walls.

After much searching, I ended up settling in a condo complex in West Hollywood—Weho, as it's known to the locals. It's nestled between Hollywood and Beverly Hills and is to Los Angeles what Chelsea is to New York City: a mecca for gay life. In Weho there are more pretty boys than you can shake a stick at. Even city hall has a pride flag outside.

Maybe it was a kind of safety zone for me. After Miami, I needed a break from relationships and men. I needed time to think about myself and learn to feel content and complete as an individual. West Hollywood provided a time-out. At least it seemed that way.

West Hollywood was indeed welcoming and fun. Everyone seemed to be in a good mood all the time. The smiling pedestrians that stepped into crosswalks like blind people, seemingly oblivious to oncoming traffic, the sometimes alarmingly altered waiters and waitresses that served patrons with collagen-enhanced smiles, and gregarious drycleaners that loved to dish as well as clean clothes, all of them bounced along as if they were whistling "Dixie."

But the stars of the city, the belles of the ball, were the guys that called Weho home. These men stared down an often disapproving world and demanded their constitutional right to pursue happiness. They had the courage to follow their hearts, found Weho, raised a rainbow flag, and created a thriving social and commercial community that welcomed all. In Weho, I would become friends with a gaggle of guys, and a few girls, who enriched my life with so much love and support that I never really felt lonely and I was able to move forward with confidence. Los Angeles quickly came to feel like home.

Moving into my apartment was psychologically grounding. It was progress that I could touch, even if, at least in the beginning, it wasn't comfortable. When I moved, I did so without even a pan or glassware. All of my furniture from my apartment in Miami was in storage, waiting to be shipped to wherever I landed. The first night in my empty apartment, overlooking the pool and the inner sanctum of the condo complex, which over the next five years would play stage to dramas worthy of any Aaron Spelling miniseries, I toasted myself with a glass of wine and curled up on the carpet in front of the fireplace.

The next day I awoke to the bright Southern California sun streaming through the chinks in the vertical blinds that hung on the sliding glass door. The long white slats clanged in the morning breeze, making the light dance in spikes across the beige carpet. I pulled myself up, pushed the blinds to the side, opened the screen door and wheeled out onto my balcony. The apartment was a one bedroom with a gas fireplace on the second floor of a comfortable and attractive seventies-era building. On the other side of the complex, directly across from my apartment, was a tree with giant thorns that grew up from the lobby through an opening in the pool area. It was quite large and reached all the way to the third floor. Hummingbirds flitted about its bright purple blossoms. Pete would brand it the "don't climb me tree."

As I was admiring the unusual flora of my new home, I heard the fluid harmony of The Mamas and The Papas drifting up from the space below. The condo was built around the pool area like an amphitheatre and all sounds were amplified. I looked around to find where the music was coming from and saw an open door down on the first floor. A calico cat lay soaking up the morning sun on the cement deck around the pool. It was such a lovely vision. To hear those harmonious voices that are so synonymous with California rising up felt good. A thin blonde man walked out of the door, called to the cat, and looked up.

"Hi!" he yelled up to me, smiling.

"Hi!" I called back to him.

His name was David and he was one of the residents who would become very dear to me.

I also met another neighbor. He stopped by to introduce himself. Brian was a semi-retired guy living off his stock trades. When he caught sight of my living room campground and learned that I would be without furniture for some time, he ran home and dragged over an extra futon that he kept for guests. He would later cart over glasses and other essentials to hold me over.

God bless them both. They had no idea that they would become my dealers for soda, beer, paper towels, and other household staples that I, a terrible homemaker as a single woman, always seemed to be running out of. They never failed me when I would ring up or knock on their doors at all hours looking for a fix of Diet Coke. This was the kind of building that I moved into.

The warm sentimental feelings surrounding my move to West Hollywood were like a healing rain after a long dry season. I was more than pleased with my new home. However, in order for me to stay there and join the happy people bouncing along its sidewalks and reveling in its eateries, I needed money.

Chasing Dreams: A Test of Faith

I had some money saved and my father agreed to help back me up if I needed it. He was happy that I managed to get out of Miami and away from Jeff and was willing to do almost anything to ensure that I stayed away. But the reality was that I was unemployed and playing it by ear.

Hollywood didn't offer much in terms of well-paying jobs for the uninitiated. I had canvassed all the studios and positioned myself as talent and as someone who knew how to produce stories for television. I became master of the pitch and was well received (I was so well received, in fact, that I even had some well-known personalities pursue me romantically). It just seemed that there were no slots open on any of the programs for which I was suited, either in front of the camera or behind it. My dwindling resources necessitated a shift in tactic.

Accepting that my dream would unfold at a less rigorous pace than I had hoped, I began to look for other work. I had run a non-profit, was organized, and was an effective communicator. After much thought, I concluded that I would make a great assistant for a Hollywood bigwig. It would have the added value of putting me in close contact with decision makers and provide me with insider information. As the trusted assistant, I could keep my eyes peeled for opportunities and continue knocking on doors while I earned a living. It seemed like a clever and realistic strategy. After all, I had a degree from one of California's top universities and experience to boot. I thought it would be a snap. Who wouldn't want to hire me? Unfortunately, there seemed to be plenty of people with the same strategy and after a thorough attempt at the studios proved fruitless, I opened up the *LA Times* Help Wanted section and began to look outside of the entertainment industry.

My frustration was quickly turning into desperation. It was disheartening. After my professional success in Miami and all of the growing pains that went along with leaving Jeff, I thought that my life would be less complicated. I felt that it would more or less unfold after I removed the impediments to growth. It was clear to me that I was talented and that people were drawn to me. I didn't understand why the charm that got me into Berkeley and a place on television seemed to be falling short now that I was focused. My finances were dwindling and I could no longer afford to wait for the world to come around to my vision of how things should unfold. With stoic pragmatism, I adjusted my strategy further.

We have all heard of the days that try men's souls. Well, for me, my first six months in Los Angeles were trying days. When we are young, we tend to look at the world with optimism and vigor and hold the belief that once we focus ourselves, anything is possible. Our parents tell us so and hopefully our educators encourage us to aim high. We are made to feel exceptional, like we are prodigies, and it creates the expectation that the world will logically understand this and make way for us accordingly.

I was in my early thirties when I arrived in California and had never struggled to be recognized in terms of my professional value before. Work came easy to me because I knew how to sell myself and could deliver on my promises. When I found myself shut out of almost every opportunity in Los Angeles, I was shocked. I never considered the possibility that I might not be able to support myself.

It was a period of uncertainty that made me think back to Saroja and the precarious days just before and after the fall of the Soviet Union. I realized that I had not been able to fully appreciate their plight because I had never wanted for anything at that time; my subsidies were never in question. Now, I was more or less on my own. My parents were there if I really needed them, but I was like a state company that the government wanted to get in shape and privatize as quickly as possible in order to be free of the burden. I remember how Saroja made hard decisions and realized that I would have to do the same. Like him, I would have to find a way to get by through whatever means necessary and keep my identity and focus intact at the same time.

How do we keep focused when things don't go they way we wish? I am not talking strictly about tragic events like my accident and my unexpected fall into abuse. Of course we will all have burdens to carry through life that we never anticipated. Here I am talking about the realization of aspirations. How do we cope when the world says you're not as good as you think you are? I believe we can either take heed and change direction or keep working towards our goals until we bring people around to our side. I chose the latter.

To do so, I knew that my commitment to my goals would have to be clear and unwavering. I took out a piece of paper and made a contract with myself. I wrote:

I, Carlana Stone, will do whatever is necessary to become a star.

Star was such an all-encompassing word. To me, being a star was just as much about standing proud and confident as an independent person as it was about being successful in the entertainment world.

I signed the note and taped it to the door of my empty freezer. With my promise to myself articulated and tangible, I set out to get work. I sent out resumes to fifty companies. Nothing. Not even a bite. I even tried calling news stations, though I had vowed not to go back to reporting. As time ran out on my finances, I began to peruse the more unexplored and exotic pages of the classifieds section. With my head held close to the page, I scoured the paper, trying to grasp the meaning of words I hadn't ever encountered in a want ad. I eventually landed on an ad under the heading of telephone sales, which was fairly self explanatory. I phoned and spoke to a man about the position. He seemed friendly and legitimate and we agreed to meet. Two days later I was finally employed.

My arrival in Tinsel Town did not create a stir in the entertainment world. I didn't swoop in like a hawk and take my rightful spot on the walk of fame. It would not even be particularly graceful. Mine would be an arrival tempered by a test of my will. I, Carlana Stone, the girl who would be the next Oprah, became a telemarketer.

Working It: Getting Past No

It's not as bad as it sounds really, telemarketing. There is a general perception that telemarketers are a sleazy bunch that will stop at nothing to annoy you into purchasing a product or service. There are definitely some culprits out there who fit the perception. But the person on the phone is someone just trying to get by. Someone like me. To this day I blow my friends minds because I actually engage in civil dialogue when I receive a call from a telemarketer. I know what it's like and that they're getting paid for the time they keep me on the phone.

Back then though, I was grateful for the work and I put myself into it wholeheartedly. While the money I made from telemarketing didn't allow for a grand lifestyle, it did enable me to manage. I was surviving. Fortunately for me, there were people around me, new friends that I met in my building and good ole' Pete and Ed, who gave my life richness. I was truly like Saroja and the Russians, getting by and banking on the future. Everyone contributed in their own small way to the reinforcement of my dream.

Brenda and I talked to each other almost every day. She helped me stay positive and I helped her by listening to her frustrations and trials of being a single mother. She was still very much part of my support structure. So were Pete and Ed and some of the people I met in my apartment building. While I was a telemarketer, I continued to knock on doors to try and gain access to the world of talk TV. I had joined a kind of support group for people trying to break in to the entertainment business and we would share information and pool resources. Whenever a new piece of information came my way, I pursued it like a like a terrier digging its way into a rabbit hole.

Around my fifth month in LA I received some information about the executive producer of Leeza Gibbons's talk show. I'll call him EP. I knew the name of the studio and even had an unconfirmed report of the name of the building his office was in. In addition, I knew that my background in human-interest reporting would be a great fit.

I mulled over my approach to the target like a CIA operative. The organization to infiltrate was Paramount Studios. My plan would involve sneaking past the guards at the gate and then, once on the lot, getting some unwitting coconspirator to point out the building in question. I would do the rest on my own.

I wasn't too concerned with the guards. I figured that I would pull a look-at-me-poor-girl-in-a-wheelchair routine and get by. Driving down Melrose towards Hollywood I got my story straight. It wasn't long before the imposing white gates of

Paramount Studios came into view. I slowed down and turned in, generating a confident smile, flashing my pearly whites.

"Good morning, y'all. How y'all doin?"

"How can I help you?" the guard asked me, giving my old Jeep Cherokee the once over.

"I have a meeting over at the Bonner Building this morning."

"Who are you seeing?"

I gave him the name of my prey and before he could call to check out my story, I hit him with the heavy artillery.

"Listen, I'm in a wheelchair and I'm not familiar with the parking around here. Is there handicap parking nearby where I need to go?" I asked in a soft pleading voice, my eyes wide with hope that I wouldn't have to struggle with any formidable obstacles like curbs or long distances. I was going for the fragile gaze of a damsel in a silent movie. He had no way of knowing that under my sexy blouse I had arms of steel and could probably take him at arm wrestling if challenged.

He looked in my back seat at the jumble of black metallic bars and padding, which gave merit to my story. As anticipated, his entire demeanor changed. His shoulders relaxed and his words were spoken in a consoling tone, as if he was speaking to someone that had recently experience the loss of a family member.

"Oh, well the building's just over there," he said. I could tell that he wanted to call me honey or dear. "And there's handicap parking nearby here. Why don't you park your car in visitor parking and I'll take you over to the building and show you where it is."

"Why thank you. Aren't you sweet?" I said, laying on my most humble and sugary Louisiana accent.

"My pleasure," he replied.

I parked and he actually escorted me to the building. The poor guy. He never knew he was being duped, but even if he did he would be heartened by the eventual outcome. Besides, it was all just in the cosmic scheme of things. Hollywood had decided to play hard ball with me and I was just returning the serve.

Once inside the Bonner building I found my way to EP's office. Like my experience at King World months before, I made my way inside to the dismay of his assistant in the reception area. This time, however, luck would be on my side.

"Hi!" I said. You have to understand that my "hi" is not your average "hi." My "hi" is a warm southern embrace that, when combined with my chair, is utterly disarming. Very few people have sufficient defenses to thwart the power of my "hi." I may not make it to my ultimate goal, but I'm rarely stopped before I have a chance to make my case.

I explained who I was and gave him my spiel. He told me, not surprisingly, that EP was very busy at the moment and wouldn't have time to see me. To his consternation, I told him that I would wait. Once again, he didn't have the heart to toss a wheelchair-bound girl out into the street. Besides that, I had a good feeling about the guy. He was young, maybe in his twenties, and I could tell that he was a West Hollywood boy.

It didn't take long for me to strike up a conversation. EP never made a showing that day, but I ended up chatting away with his assistant until we made plans to go out for margaritas at Marix, a cute little Mexican restaurant about a block away from my house on North Sweetzer in West Hollywood. It was a popular spot on Sunday nights.

I felt kind of bad about making plans to go out with him. Clearly EP was the motivating factor behind the engagement. He knew it too but we both enjoyed each others' company. We both knew that it was Hollywood and you had to be hungry if you wanted to make it. At best we might have been friends and at the very least he would have helped someone whom he felt deserved a shot. Either way I made a critical connection. The gatekeeper liked me. I knew that it was only a matter of time before I would get chance to pitch myself.

We went out and I got the rundown on Paramount and EP. He was forthcoming. Basically, EP was involved in the development of many well-know television programs and had powerhouse friends at all the other talk shows. My mouth watered at the potential. *Just one shot*, I thought. *Just fifteen minutes*. He agreed to call me on a "good" day and set something up for me. Christmas had come early that year.

I continued telemarketing. I couldn't help but think about my upcoming meeting as I dialed the numbers and pitched my product to potential customers. EP's assistant and I chatted briefly over the next week or so, sending emails back and forth. I waited. Across the roofs, just a couple miles from my building, Hollywood towered, like the formidable peak in the Paramount trailers. I waited for an opening like a mountaineer anticipating a break in the weather. I had a good feeling about this attempt. I was so close that I could taste it.

I received the call on a weekday morning. I was getting ready to go to work, for anther day of smile and dial.

"Today's a good day," he told me. It was time.

"Awesome, I'm there," I said.

When I arrived at Paramount, this time the guard recognized me and he waived me inside the gate with a "have a great day."

"I will."

As I made my way over to the Bonner building, I surveyed my surroundings. I just knew that something was going to come out of it.

I had to wait a few minutes before I could see him. But when I did, it was love at first sight. We got along fabulously. I explained that I wanted to have my own show one day, but that I was also interested in working on a talk program to learn the ropes, to learn how they put it all together and make it work. We reviewed my resume and I highlighted my experience reporting in Miami. He listened and remarked that I didn't have any program-production experience. I asked him to take a chance on me, to just give me one shot so that I could prove myself to him. He suggested that we take a walk over to meet with the supervising producers at the *Leeza* show.

What was already a great day got even better over at *Leeza*. The people on the show were wonderful. As with EP, I got along great with them. I had the feeling, as I did in the newsroom in Miami, that I belonged. Things went so well that I was convinced they were going to offer me a job right then and there. But alas, they didn't. Still, I smelled victory. I left Paramount convinced that a break had finally come my way.

Driving back to my apartment, I was frantic with thoughts of my next move. Hollywood was on the defensive. I just needed one final push and it would be mine. My hands gripped the steering wheel tightly as I mulled over the events of the day. But what to do next?

Back in my apartment I paced in my wheelchair trying to figure out a way to put myself over the top and get them to make an offer. Anything, I would do anything, as long as it had something to do with producing the kind of TV I hoped to do one day. But first, I called EP's assistant that night and thanked him from the bottom of my heart. He was thrilled for me and shared my optimism.

Over and over I thought of ways to say thank you and to plead one last time that EP take a chance on me. I needed to push without pushing so hard that I turned them off. It had to be something that was playful to reflect the casual nature of our meeting, yet told him that I had the moxie, to use Pete's favorite word, to go after what I wanted. It was going to take something optimistic. It was going to take Abba.

Yes folks, I shamelessly employed the nostalgic upbeat music of a seventies super group in my quest for success in Hollywood. Where else could one ever hope to exploit such rich material? I made a tape of the song "Take a Chance on Me" and sent it off to EP along with a note thanking him for his time and consideration.

I expected the supervisors at *Leeza* or EP himself to call with an offer immediately. Everything looked different. The sun, the trees, the sky. All of it had the incandescence of victory. Instead, EP called to thank me for the tape and said that he would keep his eye open for me if a spot opened at one of the shows at the studio. I tried to appear thankful but inside I was crushed. I couldn't believe that it didn't work. I couldn't believe that I wasn't going to get a break. Regretfully, resentfully, I went back to my job in telemarketing. I hadn't really ever left it. Mentally, however, I had finally scaled the peak and graduated to better times.

It took one more month of calls. One month more of trying to keep the faith. And then it happened. I received a call from the *Leeza* show informing me of an associate producer position that they thought I would be perfect for. Hollywood had finally caved. It was a small victory in the big scheme of things, but it was a critical step towards realizing my dream. My victory proved that if we are honest with ourselves about our abilities and have the strength and the stamina to carry the burden of our aspirations, we will usually find our way. And when we do it feels great.

I cannot ever hope to express the feeling of pride that I felt when I called my friends and family and told them about the job. I was proud for myself and also proud that I didn't let them down. When you embark on a great journey towards a lofty goal, it is almost as if you're carrying the hopes and dreams of your loved ones along with you. My parents were so pleased. My dad was relieved that my plan was showing signs of success but I could tell that my mom understood how important this victory was for me after everything that had happened. When I called Brenda, she hooted and howled so loud I'm sure that half of Miami heard her. They were all right along side me and savored my victory as if it were their own.

Breaking Through: When Life Catches up with Hope

Joining the *Leeza* show remains one of my proudest professional victories. It was my first: my first TV show, my first self-initiated breakthrough. Once I was on staff and working as an associate producer, I was teamed with talented people who spoke my language—a kind of shorthand that reflected a shared experience of the world. They all understood the kind of programming concepts that I wanted to explore. In many ways, they confirmed that the path that I had chosen was the right one. They were a resounding "yes" to the question of my chosen direction.

Leeza Gibbons was a dream. She was a true professional and took time to get to know all of us on staff. I helped put together shows that dealt with timely hot-button issues. If we were organizing a show on teen drug use, it was my job to ferret out people who would be willing to share their experiences with America. I was great at it. People found my accent disarming and I was able to put them in a place that made sharing their story a little less frightening and even an enjoyable and valuable experience.

I wouldn't put together my own shows at *Leeza*, but the experience was invaluable because I learned how talk TV functioned. A show topic was discussed and then producers were assigned to bring in real people to talk with the host about the issue. We would try to find people that would respond well to the camera and draw viewers in. After watching it all come together, I was more confident than ever that one day I might be able to produce and host my own show if I really wanted it.

This was a period of blossoming; a time when all my hard work since the accident and all the hard choices since Miami were beginning to pay off. I was independent and was finding my way through life as a single woman. I wasn't seeking anyone to complete me or act as a mirror that would validate me. I had people around me that gave my life meaning and substance. The group of friends that I made in West Hollywood gave me love and support. Now, rather than feeling part of someone, I felt like I was a part of the fabric of a community—one that I had helped to create. Each of us brought something special to the table and I reveled in the diversity and plain fun of living a life that I could be proud of. A life that felt complete.

After just one year in Los Angeles I had cleaned house. I had addressed many of the angry and dark feelings about my recent past with Jeff. It wasn't spotless. It wasn't as if I gathered all the hurt into neat bundles, wiped my hands, and shook my head in astonishment at the preposterousness of my mess like June Cleaver cleaning up after the Beaver. I was still the woman who ached and mourned at times for the girl who was lost at seventeen: the girl with dreams of playing college sports and hanging on the arm of leading men. That loss was in many ways like a death. You never really stop hurting, but you learn to live with pain and through it, hopefully, gain insight and appreciation for the value of your life and the people who give it meaning.

I had always fantasized about skydiving. I always believed that it would allow me to cheat the laws of nature, if only for a few seconds, and feel weightless and unbound to my chair. During this time period, I finally did it, making a tandem jump with an instructor on a bright sunny day over the farms of central California. He had to duct-tape my legs to his because I had no way to control them during the fall or the landing. But when we jumped out of that plane I felt a freedom and a lightness that I hadn't know since I was seventeen. It was a cathartic rush. I jumped away from Miami, away from my mistakes, and towards a fertile new land.

During those early days in Los Angeles self-love stopped being a concept and became part of my spirit. We all know what it is like to read about something, to understand and even respect it conceptually, and then to master it. When we master a certain skill or process, it is almost as if the knowledge merges with our DNA: we live and breathe it. That was the paradigm shift. From psyche to soul. It was fundamental. I was able to accept the pain as a part of me and know through and through that I was not ugly or unlovable. I made peace with the body I inhabited and the woman I had become. It showed through a smile that came from deep inside, in the way I crossed the street and said hello to passersby and in the way I worked everyday.

Making a Name for Myself

In Hollywood, nothing lasts forever. Shows come and go before they even really have a chance to fail. Six months after joining the show, they announced that *Leeza* was not going to be renewed. She had a long, successful run and I had joined her at the tail end of it. While I was sad to leave such a great bunch of people, not to mention a little concerned about the financial ramifications, I felt confident that I could find another position. I knew that I could make the grade. Like so many other industries, the trick is getting your foot in the door.

Though I was literally only on the show for a few months, word had gotten around about me. I was the least seasoned associate producer at *Leeza*, but I had made my mark in just a few months. I was known as the new girl who could convince guests that sharing their dirty laundry was in everyone's best interest. So I was honored when I became one of only three staff members from *Leeza* to get hired by *Judge Judy*. It was another Paramount show. I had a great interview with the executive producer of the show and had rave reviews from my superiors at *Leeza*. Once I was picked up so quickly, I knew that I was on my way.

Judge Judy was fun. She really is the feisty lady that she appears to be. You could respect her because she wasn't acting. She would go head-to-head with anyone when she believed in her point of view. She also wasn't a prima donna and would sometimes join me in the lunchroom and chat.

I was reprimanded on a number of occasions at *Judge Judy* by my senior producer for getting too close to my guests. I would sit in the control booth while my show was being taped and cry as Judge Judy administered the verdict in her own trademark, take-no-prisoners manner, admonishing my guests for their lack of moral fiber. And it's true, I did get close to my guests, something that is frowned upon in Hollywood because they say that it affects the way you produce. But I believe that you can't have it both ways. It's like anything else in life. If you put yourself out there and connect with people, you're going to have a meaningful experience. This is what gives my life richness and makes my work good. I have been hired over and over again for one reason and one reason only: because I know my guests inside and out and can get them to trust me and do almost anything.

While I was working at *Judge Judy,* an entertainment phenomenon was coalescing in the form of a petite, middle-aged, brassy blonde with a sharp tongue. Her name is Dr. Laura Schlesinger and she was out on the airwaves, as she is today, laying down her conservative dogma. This was when she was starting to get national recognition and just before her ill-fated TV show. Living in West Hollywood, with so many liberal people around me, you can only imagine the public outcry against her views and their impact on the national discourse on social issues.

I was offered a job at *Dr. Laura* because a lot of the people from *Leeza* had gone over there. They called and begged me to leave *Judge Judy* and even offered me a chance to field produce, which represented a big step up. It was a tough decision. I didn't agree with Dr. Laura most of the time and I still recall the horrified looks when I told the guys in my condo that I was going to be working on her show.

These people were no strangers to the rigors of Hollywood and all had stories of friends or acquaintances that compromised their integrity in order to get ahead. My compromise was actually one of the more respectable and pedestrian varieties compared to the sordid tales that they told.

There was always someone around who would speak in my defense, saying something like, "She's just doing it for the experience and then she'll get the hell out of there, right?" Then they'd look at me and take on the menacing stare of a mob boss waiting for a member of the gang to fall in line.

"Yeah, I'm outta there as soon possible," I'd say, complying as best I could.

I took the job even though *Judge Judy* was a sure thing because the show was so popular. When *Dr. Laura* was cancelled after just a couple of months I was more relieved than anything else. She and I had a lot of run-ins. Unlike her bristly persona made famous by her radio show, she never seemed to put herself out on a limb with her viewpoints when she was on camera. But she respected me because I stood up for my guests and I stood up for what I believed in. So many, junior and senior staff alike, kiss-up to hosts even if they are not performing or simply behaving badly. In fact, as time went on, Dr. Laura seemed unable to handle the tempest she had created. Most of my friends were thrilled.

Word continued to spread about me and I kept getting offers. I took another job with a reality show called *Talk or Walk*. *Talk or Walk* was a program that brought two feuding parties together. The host, a motivational speaker, made them agree to talk their issues through or walk away from each other for good.

There, at *Talk or Walk,* my flakey producer provided me yet another opportunity to stand out from the crowd. When my producer dropped the ball, I stepped up to the plate and got the job done. When you produce for talk shows or reality TV, it's your job to find real people who are willing to share their story in public and will react well to the studio environment. You look for those folks who are not going to be afraid to air their dirty laundry to the world. It's what makes good TV.

I was promoted to producer and stayed on the show for about a year, all the while improving my skills. I gained a great deal of studio experience while working at these shows and all the while continued growing into myself. My life was like a freight train; once I got moving in the right direction there was no stopping me.

It wasn't long before I earned a job producing a reality show for FOX. It was my first primetime gig and I was so proud. I learned so much and was promoted to senior producer! That meant that I had a lot of say over the direction of the programs. I've been known to pluck my guests right off of a park bench or a bar stool and talk them into doing a show about their love lives, family issues, etc. A guest who fails to appear is probably the scariest thing for a producer. I was always the one who could fill the holes for the other producers at the last minute.

My success in Hollywood mirrored the solid personal gains that I had made since leaving Miami. I worked hard at the studio and focused on living a sober life. By that I mean I wasn't just moving forward in a rush. I didn't just go along with the flow or blast through my days without stopping to think about where I was and where I was going. I was, in a very real way, trying to stay aware of my past mistakes and live my life in a way that would help reinforce good habits. Habits that reflected notions of self-worth and respect, which were independent from my relationships, be they with friends, family, or partners, yet which helped to shape them.

As I grew into the person that I had always aspired to be, one who was forthright and truthful with herself and everyone around her on all levels, I began to call into question the ethics of some of the reality TV programs that I was involved with or asked to join. I felt like we were taking vulnerable people and exploiting their weaknesses for entertainment. But it would be some time before I took action on this front. Before that would happen, all of my personal training would come to fruition in the form of a loving relationship.

The Road to Success Is Often Traveled Alone

It took a leap of faith to pick myself up from Miami and move to a new city in order to pursue a dream. When I look back at the dark period I had just come out of, faith was all I really had left: Faith in my friends and family to be there for me when I needed them. Faith in myself, in my abilities and my capacity to learn from my mistakes. I had to believe that I could still achieve something wonderful and that the grace of my success would not be limited to the workplace.

Sometimes, all you can do is move forward, armed with a little knowledge and a dream. For me, staying in Miami would have meant never really giving my dream of success in Hollywood a shot. No matter what happened, I had to try. There were people who said that I might have been dreaming too big. The idea that I could roll into Hollywood armed with just a recommendation letter from General Norman Schwarzkopf was a long shot in most people's books. After I moved to Los Angeles and things didn't pan out as I hoped at first, these same people recommended that I start thinking about other options. I stood firm.

We are all the masters of our own dreams. I was the only one who knew how good I could be, and that moving to Los Angeles was more than just about pursuing a career in Hollywood. To me, it was the simple act of creating my own future. In the end, I was able to use my pain to realize my dream:

BE WILLING TO BEAR THE BURDEN OF YOUR DREAMS

If you have put your dream on hold, whether it is a new career or changing your life in some fundamental way, it is never too late.

Take the time to research what you want to do. Once you find out all you can, be honest with yourself. Ask yourself if you really have the skills or the personality traits needed to go after your dream.

There are many tests that you can take. There is the famous Myers Briggs personality test that is supposed to give you an indicator of the careers that you are best suited for. But there is no substitute for guts and determination. Someone who has raw talent and who is dedicated to achieving a goal can go far, even if they have to work harder in the beginning to get started. I know plenty of people in Hollywood, myself included, who fit that category. Bottom line: if you want something bad enough, don't let anyone—mother, father, friends—deter you.

Arm yourself with knowledge and honesty and then make a map between where you are and where you want to be. The burden is on you, and if you give your dream a sincere attempt, there can really be no failure no matter what the outcome.

Living Proof: *Surviving Infidelity*

Danny and Melissa were married for seven years. Right out of college, the world was their oyster. They supported each other's dreams of building the perfect home. While Danny's business was booming, Melissa kicked in with her know-how to keep the books. They were great partners. They eventually had a little girl and later a boy. Melissa stayed at home to raise the kids and do her part. Danny traveled a lot with his new booming business. It was while he was away on business that Melissa found out that Danny had been unfaithful. Her heart broke and her world crumbled.

When adultery shatters a relationship, both partners lose something. The betrayed feel as if they will never be able to trust or love wholeheartedly again. The betrayers feel they will never again find such flawless, undemanding love from the one they hurt.

Both sides must mourn these losses before they can change and move on. Like any grief, the sorrow for a dead relationship goes through stages: denial, anger, guilt, and acceptance. All stages must be experienced before couples can find forgiveness and rebirth. The process requires great courage, determination, and stamina. You cannot forgive and reform your life while you are ruled by resentment, bitterness, and hurt. You can't deny your emptiness, although a sad number of people try to do so.

Allow yourself to grieve for your old relationship.

First of all, the betrayer must agree to stop the adulterous affair in order to rebuild the marriage. No change in the relationship can occur as long as one partner keeps running to an escape hatch.

Do not, however, dwell in the past, sighing about how wonderful things used to be. Obviously, matters were not perfect or no affair would have taken place!

Danny and Melissa were open and willing to bear the burden of their dreams of a perfect marriage. They are in counseling still but make time for each other and have taken this opportunity to learn from the experience. They each found that the other was feeling unsatisfied about different aspects of their relationship. They are closer than they ever dreamed possible and each knows how important they are to each other. Melissa and Danny are living proof that if we stay true and are willing to bear the burden of our dreams, we can make it last.

Dream on!

In this exercise, sit down with a recorder if you have one; otherwise a pen and paper will work fine. Dream and fantasize about your where you would like to be in three yeas.

Let it flow, be extravagant with your vision, and replay it over and over again. Then pick out the reality and keep a hint of risk. After you have talked it through with yourself, thinking of the obstacles and how to overcome them, make still another recording of WHAT I AM GOING TO DO, BY WHICH DATE, and determine to TELL YOUR BEST FRIEND or the closest person to you.

Recording helps in several ways. First, it'll serve as a reminder and you'll hear your own voice making a commitment. The written word is not as good, but will serve the same objective. Also, to verbalize it to one other person helps to make you accountable. The key here is to begin to see that you can do it! *So go do it!*

CHAPTER 11

Taking a Vow

● ●

A Nest to Call Home

Living in West Hollywood, I was surrounded by plenty of men who were happy as clams to be on their own. Not that they wouldn't be open to a relationship if the right gal came along, but they were content living on their own and sharing their lives with friends. Women are different. We are driven to nest. Some of it might be social constructs that present us with an image of success, which includes marriage and children. However, I think that we are hardwired to want to share our lives with someone special, to build a comfortable and safe space to grow.

There are lots of things that can get in the way, but by and large we women are striving to live up to the example of parrots and penguins, animals that mate for life. Coming out of my miserable experience, I was leery of trying to build a nest again. I didn't want to make the same mistake and turned down many suitors during my first year in LA. I wanted to be sure that I had a handle on myself, that I was secure enough with my condition to ensure that I could share myself. More importantly, I looked for someone who was equally in touch with himself. The last nest I made was flawed and it fell apart, almost destroying me in the process. I wanted the next one to be strong and beautiful. About a year after my arrival in LA and making my way in Hollywood, I felt I was ready, for the first time ever, to build a relationship.

My old friend Pete plays bass for a band called the Rumblebees, a group of talented musicians who bring wit and humor to rock 'n' roll. I had seen them play at a bar on the Santa Monica Pier several times and taken notice of their drummer. He was a fit, forty-something looking man with salt-and-pepper hair. After one of their shows, I made an inquiry and found out his name was John Lawson and that he was recently separated.

One Saturday afternoon I was invited to a studio in Hollywood to watch the band record its first CD. I sat in the control booth as they played their songs. It was cool being able to see how they put it all together. I kept an eye on John as he banged away on the drums and even spent a few moments chatting with him in the booth between songs.

Later that night I drove home to West Hollywood and reflected on the past year. There was Miami and then there was LA. The two cities stood in opposite relief of each other, yet were connected like the Greek masks of Tragedy and Comedy. Darkness and light. Between them, events strung out over an arch of time like stars in a constellation. In one year, I had totally extricated myself from Jeff. An acquaintance of ours who passed through LA offered me an envelope containing a letter from him. I asked him to take it back. I didn't even want to open it. I'm told that Jeff flew into a rage at the sight of the unopened letter, a tangible sign of my rejection of him and the person I was then. I wasn't going to play his game any longer.

The most marked change, the one that made me feel like all the struggling was worth it, was the greater sense of control that I had over my life and the peace that I had made with myself. I had forgiven myself for my mistakes. For getting in the car that night all those years ago. For Jeff. Out of my pain came a deeper understanding of myself and a desire to heal, which I had learned would be an ongoing process. It was as if as I was in my own twelve-step program that required vigilance and a little work each day.

I don't want to give the impression that life was perfect. There's always something popping up when you least expect it to challenge your progress and momentum. But the deep-rooted need for acceptance that led me into the arms of an abuser was acknowledged. And bringing it out into the open drained a lot of the energy from it. It was like a festering wound that was finally beginning to scab over and heal in the warmth of the sun.

I was living my life on my own and didn't *need* a man to make me feel whole. There were plenty of good friends around me. Still, I liked the idea of sharing my joy with someone special and missed the intimacy that comes with any relationship. I liked the way John smiled when I came in the room and his youthful nature. He had the posture of man who was confident without being cocky. His voice was kind and rarely the loudest in the room. I didn't know the details of his separation but, and perhaps I was projecting, I thought I could see a hint of sadness in his eyes at times. I respected him for the sentiment, because it meant that he was a man that felt deeply for the things in his life. In general, from what I knew of him, he was a good man. I decided that I would ask him out.

I had never asked anyone out before. Men had always come to me. It had been a measure of my attractiveness. Waiting for a phone call from a man was precisely the kind of behavior that I needed to change. If, from the get-go, I was the one reaching out and putting myself on the line because I found the person attractive, it would mean that I was taking a proactive role. I didn't want to be the one waiting to be chosen and validated any longer.

The day I called John I was a nervous wreck and half hoped that he wouldn't answer the phone.

"Hi. It's Carlana," I said, trying to mask the nervousness in my voice.

"Well hey there," he said, his voice rising in surprise. He sounded more excited than I had ever heard him before. I took it as a good sign.

I found myself engaged in warm-up conversation. I was normally on the receiving end of these calls and empathized with all the guys that had asked me out over the years. It's so awkward! Getting out the invitation can be like passing a kidney stone.

"Well, I was wondering if you were busy on Friday. I though we could have dinner or something?"

He enthusiastically accepted and we made plans to go out for dinner. On Friday night he met me at my apartment. Neither of us knew that it was a date with destiny.

We had both been out of the dating scene for a while. I had waited an entire year, but John was really rusty. He was just coming out of a twenty-year relationship. Still, he arrived on Friday evening and we went out to dinner. There was the usual lighthearted conversation that goes along with first dates and we each tried to look good. He told me about his career as a sound engineer at Warner Brothers. He complimented me and his eyes kept wandering from my face to other areas. It felt good to know that he found me attractive, but I was interested in more than his approval. I was interested in him.

Because we were older and had been through the wringer in terms of relationships, we were both forthcoming. He was a sensitive, straightforward man whose life had unraveled a few months earlier. Married for twenty years, he and his wife separated; a separation that he initiated but nonetheless drained him emotionally. He was the father of two high school-aged children whose pictures he carried around in his wallet. After twenty years of fatherhood and marriage, he was slowly becoming acclimated to single life. But the things that initially attracted me to him, his easygoing, gentle way, appeared genuine. He turned out to be very much the man that I envisioned, only better.

A private pilot, he owned his own plane, which he built himself. He carried a picture of himself and the plane around and showed it off as if it was a third child. At the end of the evening, he brought me home and we said our goodbyes. The other crucial ingredient made itself known as we had a glass of wine on my couch—we had chemistry. He was a good kisser to boot.

He left me with a photo. I didn't get flowers or chocolate, but I got a picture of man and his airplane. Later I would learn that the picture told a thousand words about John Lawson. He didn't just fly planes, he built them. It would take many days and nights spent together for me to understand all the meaning wrapped up in his photo and how much we had in common.

Learning to Love Again

Airmen. The daring guys who challenge nature and fly. For serious pilots, flying is like a form of meditation. They revel in the ability to briefly leave the earth and be above it all, literally and metaphorically. When they are in command of an airplane, they reach beyond the scope of human experience. They are free.

Good pilots, like John, are respectful of their passion. He keeps his zeal in check so that he does not become a modern day Icarus. John is methodical, employing a mind-boggling attention to detail that ensures he doesn't put himself or anyone else in danger. There is always a degree of risk when those wheels leave the ground at over 100 mph, but John is mindful of his actions and measured in his response to the conditions in which he finds himself. This has come from years of training. He has learned what weaknesses he might have that would make him vulnerable to certain kinds of mishaps. He understands how rough air and unexpected weather are best managed. And he knows how his airplane, an extension of himself in the air, is best handled.

I believe that John's love of flying and the lessons that come with being an airman helped him to get through his separation. So many of the concepts and ideas that pilots use are applicable on a personal level. We are all flying our own aircraft in some way, trying to get to wherever we are going safely and in control. We are all trying to enjoy the journey. Flying taught John the value of checking and double checking things, of getting to the bottom of the dullest rattle before it grew into something dangerous. Of challenging assumptions and knowing your limits. John worked his way from sadness and loss to a place that allowed him to accept the past, understand his merits and faults, and permit the entry of something new.

In that way, John Lawson and I were a lot alike. Over time, John and I shared the details of our lives with each other. My accident. My past with Jeff. He told me about his marriage and how things had gone wrong. We were both honest with each other and helped each other grieve. Finding someone who speaks your language is like finding the Holy Grail. Probably the most beautiful aspect of our budding life together was the lack of need. John and I didn't need one another. We each had plenty of opportunities to date if we wanted them. We chose to be with each other because we understood where we had come from and saw the potential for a partnership, one which would take us both to new heights.

He and I fell into a life together easily. I grew to know his children and even his ex-wife. The kids are wonderful. I love children and could have them if I wanted. However, I am honest enough with myself to know that motherhood is just not something that I am best suited for. Having two instant teens to get to know and love was a blessing.

Eric and Stephanie embraced me from the beginning. I look back on those first months with great fondness because even then I felt that I was laying the groundwork for a lifetime of memories.

Around a year after we started dating, John and I took a serious step and moved in together. It was a big moment for both us, but it felt right. He was spending most of his time at my house in West Hollywood anyway and he worked in Hollywood, which was just a few minutes from my apartment. From the very beginning, things went well. He supported me in my desire to move beyond producing television to be in front of the camera. I supported him in his own career, in his relationship with his children, and took up the hobby of airplanes. We spent most of our free time out at the airfield where he keeps his plane. I became a trusted navigator and we would often take short trips up and down the California coast, sometimes landing and camping out for the night under the stars.

My parents and sisters took to John immediately. After what had happened in Miami, they were eager to see who was in my life. But after just one visit to LA, they realized that John was nothing like Jeff. Moreover, I think that they understood that I was different too. I wasn't the same girl that I was in Miami and John was living proof that I was making decisions with a healthy soul. Even Brenda came to visit from Miami and gave her seal of approval.

We continued in this way for three years. We lived in my apartment and worked in Hollywood, growing stronger by the day. We developed the silly habits of lovers and kept discovering new dimensions of each other and in the dynamic of our relationship. There were some rough spots, there always are. On occasion we wouldn't agree on how an issue should be dealt with, but these were growing pains that both of us realized paled in comparison to our shared vision. Our vision of our life together never faltered and only grew clearer each day.

I had never imagined that my life could feel so complete. I was in love with someone and he with me. We were building a life together. There was no tug-of-war, no fighting for control. Ours was a relationship that respected the feelings and the needs of the other person. Being in a place of such honesty and adoration fed my self-confidence on a level that dwarfed all my progress up until that point. I was still me, I hadn't lost myself in John, but John's love and respect built me up and powered my growth.

One evening, after a long day at work, I came home to a wonderful meal that John prepared. Yes, the man can cook too. I was exhausted and took to the couch to relax and drink a well-earned glass of wine. John came over and kneeled on the floor in front of me. At first I didn't quite understand what was happening. He told me how much he loved me and enriched his life. And then I saw the ring. At the end of the third year together, John asked me to marry him. I said yes.

A Partnership of Equals

I couldn't believe that I was going to get married. I was thirty-five. After Jeff, I wondered if I wanted to put myself into a situation that legally bound me to someone. I just didn't like the finality of it all. But once I found John, my equal, I changed my mind. I wanted the world to know how good we were. That we had both made it. John and I were a team and our wedding would be a merger of two people that found each other despite horrendous odds and personal struggle.

We spent a great deal of time trying to plan our wedding. I wanted it to be unique and personal. We finally settled on a beautiful winery up near Santa Barbara. The woman who owned the place was originally from New Orleans and that pretty much sealed the deal. I wanted my wedding to be a fusion of Louisiana home-cooking and music and the wondrous potential represented by the California landscape. I wanted to bring both homes together. In a way, it was like I was patching my past in Shreveport to my life in California. I was nurtured in both places. Each allowed me to be free and encouraged me to grow.

The theme would be Louisiana Cajun, with cornbread, crawfish etouffe, gumbo, and all the expected staples around for everyone to feel right at home. We hired a zydeco band to play at our reception, which was held the night before the ceremony, and at the ceremony itself. We even arranged to have a Southern Baptist preacher preside, probably the only Southern Baptist preacher in Santa Barbara.

A big issue for me was the way I would enter on the day of the ceremony. I didn't want to wheel in and be at the same level as the guests. I wanted to feel like a bride standing in front of family and friends and be able to look into John's eyes as we exchanged our vows. I thought that it would be nice if I could be carried in to the ceremony in some way that was at once playful yet dignified. I wracked my brain and asked everyone I knew for ideas but a solution to my unique problem eluded me until I decided to turn to the great resource right under my nose: Hollywood.

Living in Hollywood can be useful when you're looking for the out of the ordinary prop. There are all sorts of places that hold treasures from old films waiting to be rediscovered and put to new use for a small fee. I went to one of these fantastic warehouses to search for my answer. I explained my predicament to the owner and he pondered for a moment and then proclaimed that he had just the thing.

He brought me to a corner of the vast space, past huge artifacts of Hollywood. Most of the stuff was old, from the golden era. He stopped in front of a golden chair with arms that curled under like the end of a scroll. It was more of a throne really, with a base on which the seated individual could rest their feet. He then pointed to two long black poles lying on the ground nearby. He picked one up and I caught on. The poles fit into the curl of each arm so that the person sitting could be carried about. It was a kind of palanquin.

"This is from the movie *The Ten Commandments,*" he said. "They carried Queen Nefertiti in it. This other stuff goes with it."

He dragged out two long poles with fans of fluffy white ostrich feathers attached to the top and another shorter torch-like, golden-handled baton with peacock feathers attached. All it took was the sight of all those feathers and the entire wedding came together in my head. It was a Cajun theme and what could be more Cajun than a festive, Mardi Gras-like promenade to the altar?

Our wedding took place on a glorious sunny Sunday morning in February 2004. I wore a cranberry colored suede suit and John and all the guys wore cowboy boots and black jeans. Two good friends festooned the chair with flowers that matched the color of my dress.

I thought a great deal about who would carry me in the chair to the altar. I decided that I wanted the women in my life to bring me to John. I would have my two sisters, Mitzi and Karen, and two childhood friends from Shreveport, Karen and Susan. I was desperate for Brenda to share the day with me. She of all people had a place in my wedding march. Unfortunately she couldn't make it, but I spoke to her on the day of the wedding and she gave me her blessing. My father carried the peacock torch and my two friends, John and David, carried the tall feathered poles behind us all.

The fifty or so attendees gathered on a stretch of lawn beside a great tree. After a wave of my father's hand the zydeco band began to play a sweet Cajun wedding tune and the procession started. John stood with his children at the head of the crowd, watching us as we walked under a trellis of roses and then made our way down the grassy isle to him. The sunlight was pure magic that morning, crisp and clean.

The women put the chair down and my father reached over and picked me up, placing me on the chair next to John.

The preacher started by saying, "If you ever told me that a black preacher would be performing a wedding ceremony for a white family from Louisiana in Santa Barbara, I would never have believed ya!"

John and I had both thought long and hard about our vows. Since a religious man was presiding over the ceremony, he demanded that we stick to the traditional wedding script but agreed to give us a moment at the end to say something. This was our moment to proclaim our love for each other in front of the people that had been with us throughout our engagement and courtship. Some had known us before we were John and Carlana. They had seen us both suffer and grow. That each of us had made it to that moment was a sweet victory in which most people in attendance had a share.

The preacher had us all repeat the Lord's Prayer and then let us say our pieces to each other. I looked at John and began to speak. As usual, I spoke off the cuff and poured all my feelings and sentiment over him like warm rain.

You are the embodiment of everything I've ever searched for in my life. You are true love and compassion and the most spectacular friend and lover and confidante. I am sitting here so proud to be with you and to devote the rest of my life to you because since I was a child I have dreamt of discovering true happiness and...I am positive I had never experienced what true happiness was until you walked into my life.

You have given me so much incredible strength; you have loved me and supported me in my growth and in learning to figure out who I am and where I'm going, and you've taught me how to love myself more than I've ever loved myself. And because I'm at a point where I love myself so much, it enables me to give you love and that much more love and I'm gonna spend the rest of my life loving you and holding you and cherishing you and I will never take you for granted. And I'm not...and you're not going anywhere!

I love you and I devote the absolute rest of my life to you and making you happy and making us whole. I love you.

He responded in the measured manner. A true pilot by nature.

"Since I'm not as good as winging it..." he said, opening up a folded piece of paper on which he had written a poem.

> She stands before me this woman in red. On this day to take my hand and my heart into hers for the rest of our days.
>
> And I reflect on wondrous moments these three years past, too many to recall, but too few a lifetime to fill.
>
> God first practiced a million years and then created this beautiful creature. This masterpiece of perfection. How fortunate am I to be the recipient of her love, so great and so rare. In my years I've acquired just enough wisdom so as not to question that which arrives unexpectedly.
>
> This love has known barren sands. This love has known the lush meadow. This love has survived the drought and this love has thrived in the rain.
>
> Like a blade of grass which grows out of the rock, it knows not its own strength, but just that it must live and trust that something greater will tend its need. Now we know not where our paths shall lead but we rejoice in the knowledge that we both shall from this day forward walk it together.
>
> Not one in front of the other, but side-by-side, hand-in-hand.
>
> Carlana, I will help you to your feet when you stumble. And you will carry me upon your back when I am weak. And when at last our sun sets and we breathe our last mortal breath, we will look back upon the years left to come and know that we lived happily ever after.

And then the reverend led us through our vows. John placed the ring on my finger and I said I do. Pledging my love to him, I repeated the same with John.

Vow. It is a serious word. That day, in front of our friends and family, John and I vowed to love each other until our dying day. But we really did more than that. We each vowed, in our own way, to respect ourselves as well as one another.

I vowed to never lose sight of my journey. I vowed to keep loving myself so that I could keep loving John and the people that give my life meaning. I vowed to not give up my struggle to be the best person I can be. After all those years of pushing against a mountain of doubt and pain, I had finally figured out that some things are just part of our personal landscape. And that you best assess their nature and learn to scale them rather than try to erase their presence entirely. It'll never happen. We'll all have hills and valleys. And I crossed some dangerous terrain. I tried to find short cuts and alternative routes, but in the end I took the time to understand what I was facing and made my way, step by step, over them until I was clear and on fertile ground.

Day By Bay

Since our wedding, John and I have resettled into a Spanish-style stucco home built in the twenties. Our days have a comfortable routine to them.

John is a sound engineer for a major movie studio and needs to be at work early in the morning. But no matter what, each day, lying in bed, sometimes in the dark of winter, we always take the time to talk with each other about the day ahead. We take the time to say, "I love you." And we won't leave the house without expressing how much we mean to each other. It's a small gesture, but it's a great way to start the day.

After he leaves, I'll take a bath. It's a fact of life for me. Baths are just the easiest way to get clean. Nobody I know takes baths anymore, but I think that they're a great tool for starting or ending a long hard day.

During my early days in Hollywood, I took whatever work I could get. Now I try to work for shows that I believe offer more than entertainment value. I don't want to feel like I'm exploiting someone who's suffering. I want to believe we're trying to help them get better. I'm still aggressive and go after jobs with as much tenacity as I ever did. But when I work now, I do it very much on my own terms.

Often, if I'm casting, I'll be able to work from my house. Regardless of where I am, I am always on the phone conducting interviews, gathering profiles, and arranging FedEx deliveries. There are fires to be put out over guests who are having cold feet about appearing on television. There are run-ins with executive producers. There are deadlines. My day is basically spent trying to create a meeting of the minds between guests, producers, and hosts. It's a juggling act that requires patience and tenacity. It can be maddening at times, but it's rewarding when it all comes together.

When I'm not working on a show, I do quite a bit of public speaking. I am asked regularly to speak to youth groups and professional associations. My message borrows from the themes covered in this book. Depending on who I'm speaking to, I try to tell them a story that they can relate to and which conveys an insight that I feel they can use. For example, I often speak with at-risk young adults and try to convey how important it is to be thoughtful of their actions, to reach out for help if they need it, and to understand that they are not alone.

Free time is spent with John's children, close friends, and flying. John and I have flown all over California since we met. I had jumped out of planes before I knew John. But once I was married to a pilot, I figured that I might as well learn how to fly them too. To my delight, I received flying lessons as a Christmas present and have been preparing for my solo flight. I am always looking for new challenges and experiences.

What follows is a contract that John and I have with each other. It sits on our kitchen wall and there isn't a day that goes by that I don't take a moment to look at it.

Happily Ever After
We are friends first, always
Friendship is our foundation,
the solid rock on which we are built

Our love has no agenda
We love each other without condition or expectation

We are honest
Our love knows only truth

We trust one another
Because we must. The heart knows no other path

We protect each other's heart
We are kind and gentle with our words and actions

We respect one another
We extend to each other that which we expect for ourselves

We recognize our humanity
We make mistakes, but we forgive ourselves
and each other for our shortcomings

We cherish the moment
We stay forever mindful that the past is not the present

We evolve
We continue to grow together and as individuals

We celebrate our differences
We are unique and encourage one another
to be nothing less than who we are

We protect one another
We provide a place of solace and safety in times of vulnerability

We listen to one another
To hear each other's point of view

We give
unconditionally

The View from
Way Up Here

• •

I am sitting at the foot of a long runway waiting for my takeoff clearance on what will be my first solo flight as a pilot. I believe that my learning to fly was inevitable. Between my arrival in California and my meeting John, I had skydived and experienced the freedom of freefall. But that was the best I could do then, after the devastation of Miami. Meeting John and achieving success in Hollywood on my own gave me the insight to turn freefall into controlled flight; a desperate escape into a journey with a destination.

Today, as I ready to take to the air, I can't help but reflect on how the process of learning to fly has mirrored my personal journey through life. When I was seventeen, a horrible accident threatened to steal my future. But I fought back. And so many of the lessons that I have learned in the course of overcoming my adversity are strikingly similar to those embraced by pilots trying to conquer the sky: your airplane is built to fly even after its been compromised; trust your instincts; know your limits; know when to ask for help. All those fundamental tenets resonated with me.

I am now in my mid thirties and live a very fulfilling life with my husband and soul mate. But there are times when I think back to the days of searching. I still speak with my friends from Boulder and reminisce about the old days and how far we have all come since then. Brenda continues to be a close friend and confidant. And there are still times on cold winter nights when I catch myself looking out of the kitchen window at the dark sky and thinking of Saroja and the dear people who had so little, yet wanted so much to believe in a miracle for me. I cherish them all and they will always be with me.

Racing down the runway I watch my instruments and feel the plane delicately lift off the ground. Soon I am soaring high above Southern California. Ahead are mountains and valleys. Here and there are patches of beige among the green that reveal parched earth. Seen from above, the landscape mirrors the terrain of life: verdant peaks, deep valleys, and the occasional patch of desert. A good survivalist is someone who is prepared to mitigate any environment.

Paralysis and abuse were my deserts. But I have learned along the way that paralysis comes in many forms. A divorce or the loss of a loved one can leave you emotionally paralyzed. Even the loss of a job can bring on a feeling of intense helplessness. When something that we have invested a great deal in is taken away from us—friends, family, looks, or livelihood—we are faced with the question of how to bring meaning and purpose back to our lives.

I hope that my story will serve as an inspiration for you on your journey forward, no matter what your future may hold. Adversities are challenges. We can allow them to consume us or we can use them as tools to transform our lives and become better human beings. I truly believe that my life would have been far less rich in terms of my personal growth and experiences had I not suffered my loss. I am living proof that with honesty and courage, we can excel in even the most trying circumstances. Take my insights to heart. If you dig deep, you too can find a way to transform your deserts into lush gardens.

Acknowledgments

First of all, I thank John Di Rienzo, my best friend and co-writer for agreeing to take on this challenge. I thank him for his gift of eloquence, his mastery of the written word. Like an artist, he has painted a beautiful canvas, poetry which truly expresses my innermost and deepest feelings. I knew from the beginning that there would be no other person who could possibly grasp the inner workings of my heart and soul and complicated mind. We've been best friends for half of our lives—he's been there through the highs and lows. He has lived *in* my story. We have evolved together, literally grown up together. Writing this book has been a journey, wrought with heart-wrenching and painful revelations, but the joys and triumphs always prevailed. I am forever grateful that "Johnny D" believed in me enough to take my hand and join me in this journey.

I am forever grateful to my beloved husband, John Lawson. Without him, this project would not have been possible. He is my rock. And the most beautiful man I've ever known, inside and out. One of my most gratifying moments in my life was when he said yes when I asked him out on our first date. My proudest moment was marrying him and I value him for having the courage to go through the emotional roller-coaster ride of his life. He is an engineer, a musician, and a pilot who has taken me to new heights and shown me the world from a different perspective. I thank him for hanging by my side and encouraging me to delve into the dark side of my pain; he has stood by me, and I feel my safest when in his arms. He has given me the courage to tackle even the most painful realities. He asks the hard questions of me. My husband has offered me a place of comfort and solace and been a catalyst in my discovery of true self-love and acceptance. We have grown together and share the strongest union imaginable. John has taught me the true meaning of partnership and the concept of unconditional love. He has helped me learn to sit with my imperfections and celebrates every part of who I am. And I thank him for being in my life.

I thank my mother and father, Sissy and David Stone, who provided me with this rock-solid foundation and never allowed me to fall into the state of self-pity. They challenged me without shaming me. Our family could have collapsed and fallen apart as many do when tragedy strikes, but because of the unshakable base my parents have provided, our family dynamic has been enhanced by our life experiences. As a result, we were brought closer and share a stronger sense of unity and togetherness. My sister Mitzi is a kindred spirit of whom I am so proud; she has worked so hard at raising her beautiful family. She's a nurse, which I must say is, without question, her calling, as she was born to be a caretaker. I thank her for her willingness to relive some of those difficult memories with me and for fielding those late-night phone calls. My sister Karen's and my relationship has evolved over the years, but it wasn't until this book, as I shared the words in these pages, that she said to me, "Carlana, I never really knew you before reading your book." Karen has grown into one of my biggest fans, sharing each chapter as it was completed with all of her coworkers and friends. Our relationship has grown into that bond of which I've always dreamed. That fact alone makes this entire journey worthwhile, even if we never sold a single copy.

I thank my beautiful step kids, Eric and Stephanie, who have welcomed me with open arms.

I thank all my friends who had the courage to see with their hearts, those who have stood by me before and after the accident, who were able to see past the confines of my wheelchair, and celebrate the person who dwells inside. I thank Karen Jordan, my roommate in spinal cord rehab, for her example of strength and fortitude. I thank my friends in Boulder who loved and accepted me, skinny legs and all. I treasure and honor the memory of my friend, Jordan Heminway, my partner in pain during our search for new identities. I cherish the many happy memories and the life lessons I learned from Saroja, Tatiana, and my many other friends in Russia. I thank Brenda Jove, a single mother of three and a dear friend, for her tough love approach when I needed it the most.

I thank General Norman Schwarzkopf, who really is a teddy bear at heart, and Leeza Gibbons and Ben Stein and the countless others who have realized my potential and supported my journey. They've helped open many doors in my quest to make a name for myself in the entertainment industry.

There are so many people who have influenced my life and touched my heart in so many ways that it is impossible to name you all.

We thank our agent, Alice Martel, for believing in us and having the vision and the gumption to sell this book.

We thank our editor, Hillel Black, a true gem of a man. We thank him for bringing his experience and excellent insight to this project. We cherish his invaluable contribution.

We thank Laura Gorr, Heather Otley, Michelle Schoob, Matt Diamond, and Tony Viardo and all the wonderful folks at Sourcebooks who have spent tireless hours getting this book ready for print and believing in us enough to take us out and present us to the world.